ESSAYS

REFLECTIONS ON SUCCESS, HAPPINESS AND
THE MEANING OF LIFE

THIBAUT MEURISSE

Edited by
KERRY J DONOVAN

Illustrated by
ROY PALLAS

Publisher: Self Mastery

© 2024 Thibaut Meurisse

CONTENTS

INTRODUCTION

This book is a collection of ideas, insights and reflections. It is an opportunity for me to put on paper what's on my mind. In it, I have included everything that piques my interest. I share ideas, raise questions and offer frameworks on a variety of topics such as success, happiness, money, personal development and the meaning of life.

Perhaps you have read several of my books in the past and would like a sneak peek at my thought process. Perhaps you're looking for different perspectives to cultivate your intellectual curiosity. Or perhaps you have encountered this book by chance. In any case, I encourage you to read a few paragraphs and see how you like it.

There is no specific order in which to read it. Open it at any page and start reading. I hope this book will give you a few invaluable ideas to reflect on as you navigate the complexity of life.

This book raises more questions than it provides answers. It is a summary of what I've been thinking about for a while. However, please remember I'm expressing my opinions. While I may be right in some instances, I'm likely to be wrong in others. Therefore, I encourage you to challenge everything I say and draw your own conclusions. Happy reading.

GRAB YOUR FREE BOOK

Visit *thibautmeurisse.com* and grab your free book

1

ON CONTRADICTIONS

As you read this book, you may feel as though I contradict myself occasionally. And you may be right. This is because the world is complex and nuanced.

The human brain wants to put labels on everything. It likes to create categories to help us make sense of the world. To do so, it relies on mental models. While these models are useful, they are merely our brain's attempt to explain the world. They are not actual representations of it.

In truth, mental models are merely crutches that help us navigate through an uncertain and unpredictable world. One idea may be useful in a specific season of life but counterproductive in another. One concept may be life-changing to one person but useless to another. This is why one of the most important skills we can develop might be our ability to navigate from one model, idea or concept to the next in a flexible way.

Ultimately, ideas, concepts or mental models are like keys. Sometimes, we need to try many different keys before we can open the door in front of us. Each door is unique and requires the right key to unlock it.

Holding two thoughts at the same time

To have a successful and meaningful life, we must be able to hold two or more seemingly incompatible thoughts at the same time. Below are some examples:

- *We must think both long term and short term.* We must be patient and think long term while acting each day with a sense of urgency.
- *We must have both personal agency and compassion toward others.* We must take responsibility for our lives while accepting that others can't or won't.
- *We must be chronically dissatisfied while perpetually grateful.* We must be ambitious and strive for more while appreciating all the things with which we are already blessed.
- *We must be confident while staying humble.* We must move toward our goals with confidence while learning from our mistakes.
- *We must want to change the world while accepting the status quo.* We must have the urge to make a difference while acknowledging that the world is exactly as it should be (for now).
- *We must accept failure while being determined to succeed.* We must expect many setbacks while being determined to reach our goals over time.

These are just a few examples of being flexible with our thoughts. To live a good life, we must be able to hold two apparently conflicting thoughts at the same time while remaining sane.

The "truth"

In some ways, "truth" is situational. That is, it can change from one situation to the next. Holding seemingly contradictory ideas in our mind enables us to capture that truth and make the right decision for us at the right time.

For instance, the truth for you right now may be that you need to work harder. But the truth next year could be that you should work less. Or, right now, the truth may be that you should focus on one key project. But in three months, it might be that you should juggle multiple projects.

Only you know what the truth is for you at a particular moment.

Being ready

Everything comes in its own time. Like the caterpillar, we only turn into a butterfly when we're ready to shed our old self, to let go of part of our identity—the part that used to define us.

Often, we receive insights when we're open to them. This is why the same book or piece of advice can have a radically different impact on us at different stages in our lives. For instance, for some people, they are at a stage in life where they're ambitious. Letting their fears and ego motivate them is the right path (for now). Meanwhile, others may feel the need to let go of their ego and focus more on their spirituality.

Issues arise when we ignore timing and readiness, and try to be someone we aren't. For example, it's when we:

- Try to be more ambitious than we really are after watching a motivational video,
- Portray ourselves as spiritual beings who live in the present moment while we don't understand what the concept even means, or
- Seek spiritual enlightenment to strengthen our ego rather than as a path toward more humility.

Sometimes, we're just not ready. We can't skip the line. We must let time change us and be honest with ourselves rather than deny our present reality and the needs of the moment.

2

ON SELF-AWARENESS AND PERSONAL POWER

Personal responsibility—myth or reality?

Are we responsible for everything in our lives? If so, should we be blamed for our lack of success?

Proponents of personal responsibility believe that we are all responsible for our actions. On the other hand, detractors see the concept of personal responsibility as overly simplistic at best, and manipulative at worst. They argue that this leads people to blame themselves. Furthermore, it enables politicians to escape their responsibility by attacking poor people for not working hard enough.

Both make seemingly valid points.

So, is personal responsibility just smoke and mirrors? Or is it a real thing?

Many people could improve their personal circumstances by taking more responsibility for their lives. This is a fact. However, for a variety of reasons, they don't. This is also a fact.

In short, it's hard to argue against the fact that we can change our lives. We can make better decisions that will improve our situation over time. We can read books, learn new skills, exercise regularly or eat healthier food. There is always something we can do *right now* to start changing the trajectory of our lives.

But it's also hard to argue against the fact that some people are at a massive disadvantage. They may have to spend most of their time caring for a family member. They may have chronic diseases that prevent them from working full-time. Or they may be fighting mental illness. They just don't have the resources, time or energy to make the changes they would like in their life.

In conclusion, most of us can probably change our lives. But for some it will be way harder than for others.

Changing ourselves vs. changing the system

Should we spend our time and energy trying to change the system, or should we use our valuable time to change ourselves? Over the years, I have concluded that changing ourselves is the better strategy. This is because most external changes are the results of inner changes. By changing ourselves, we can have a far greater impact on our environment than we may realize (positive or negative). And it's easier to change ourselves than to change the system. At least we have some control over our own actions.

However, we should probably try to do both.

Should we become better?

Do we have a moral obligation to become a better version of ourselves? And how much should we be willing to sacrifice to help others?

Truth is, we can always develop more skills and help more people. Now, since we can all become more useful, should we do so? And to what extent? When is enough, enough? Should we sacrifice our hobbies? Our time with our family? Our health? Where should we draw the line? Should we refuse to help one person so that we can help one hundred others?

We could help more people. The hardest part is to figure out whether we should do so and to what extent.

Change and self-awareness

Self-awareness is the prerequisite for change. If we aspire to change, we must:

- Identify our limitations,
- Understand our strengths and weaknesses,
- Shed light on the main problems in our lives,
- Expose the gap between where we are and aspire to be, and
- Recognize the negative patterns that keep repeating in our lives.

The more self-aware we become, the likelier we are to change.

Know ourselves

Knowing who we are and acting accordingly is probably the most effective strategy to living a meaningful life. Without self-awareness and continuous self-reflection, we won't find:

- What we're good at (our talents),
- What we enjoy doing (our passion), or
- What works for us (our strategy).

As a result, it's unlikely we'll be pursuing the right endeavors.

The curse of self-awareness

Once we realize we are capable of more, we can never unsee that truth. Perhaps this is why we look for excuses to justify where we are in life. We are terrified of having to deal with the heavy burden that comes with such a realization. With great power comes great responsibility. Seeing ourselves as powerless absolves us from having to take responsibility.

The ultimate human dilemma

Becoming more aware of our potential raises fundamental questions.

How should we use our time knowing that we have an almost limitless potential, but very limited time? What should we focus our energy on each day? How should we ensure that we live a meaningful life? What principles should we follow?

In short, the curse of self-awareness means that we must take responsibility for our lives. We can't lie to ourselves anymore. We can't hide.

And it's not always good news.

Changing others

We often rush into helping others without properly understanding ourselves. We want to change the world but are reluctant to change ourselves.

The problem is that it is hard to change the world. In fact, we can spend our entire life trying to change just one other person and fail. In comparison, changing ourselves is relatively easy. However, please bear in mind that, as we change ourselves, we may end up impacting the lives of countless people around us. This is why, if we ever hope to make any kind of difference in the wider world, changing ourselves is the most effective strategy.

Understanding ourselves first

As we try to overcome our fears, addictions and inadequacies, we learn more about ourselves. As we pursue meaningful goals, we will uncover our talents, skills and our unique personality. As we keep digging inside ourselves, we will slowly reveal the fundamental truths about human beings.

Developing a deeper understanding of our psychology enables us to act from a different place. To put it differently, by delving deeper and seeking to understand our unique nature (one human being), we will acquire a profound understanding of the whole (the entire human population).

By having a greater understanding of ourselves, we can start changing ourselves—and perhaps even others.

People change when…

In most cases, if we want to change people, we need to have their buy-in first. In general, people tend to change:

- When they're asked genuine questions that help reflect on what they want and care about,
- When they feel truly listened to,
- When they are inspired by someone else's behaviors and attitude,
- When they're part of a supportive environment filled with positive people who want the best for them, and
- When they have a strong desire to change because they have reached rock bottom, or they have had an epiphany.

Let's keep these points in mind if we ever hope to "change" people.

Most advice is useless

It's hard to give any sound advice to people because we seldom know enough about their lives. We don't know what issues they face, where they're coming from, what intrusive thoughts they're battling with or what their deepest aspirations are. For the same reason, it's just as difficult for others to give us effective advice.

The harsh truth is that most advice is worthless simply because it won't work for us, or for the people we offer it to.

No one is coming to save us

We often look for something outside of us to solve our issues. We want the "magic pill", the *one thing* that will make our problems go away. We believe that if we only had the missing piece of the puzzle, everything would work out for us.

But there is no magic pill.

The secret sauce that will enable us to lose weight, gain muscle mass, create a thriving business or build fulfilling relationships is…

us.

It doesn't mean we can't or shouldn't ask for help. But we must accept that, ultimately, we are the ones who must do the work.

The "magic pill"

In truth, the only magic pill might be having a positive attitude and pursuing consistent hard work directed toward the goals that matter most. Any meaningful goal will require a great deal of time and effort —probably much more than we imagine. This is how it should be. This is what makes these goals meaningful in the first place.

The burden of hard work

Every time we want someone else to solve our problems or do the work for us, we reject our personal responsibility and try to place the burden of hard work and difficult choices on other people's shoulders.

It can't be done.

Nobody can do push-ups, eat healthily or work on our side hustle for us.

Whenever we ask someone for help, we secretly hope they will do the work for us. Or, at least, we hope they will tell us their "secrets" so that we can shortcut our way to success while doing as little work as possible.

Such a desire to cheat life doesn't work.

Picking people's brains

"Can I pick your brain?" "Can I invite you for a coffee?" "Can we have a quick chat?"

When people say these words, they usually mean:

"Can you tell me everything I need to do so that I don't have to figure it out by myself using my time, energy and money?"

In other words, it's an attempt to steal other people's knowledge while having as little skin in the game as possible.

This is lazy and manipulative.

Let's remember that no one else can do the work for us. *We* must do the work. We must have skin in the game and invest our time, money and energy in whatever we say we care about.

If we can't do that, we're simply not serious about our goals.

We *can* change

We might not be able to change our immediate circumstances, but we can change what we think, eat, read, who we listen to, what intentions we have, what goals we set or how much we exercise each week. We can always change something. And as we change, sooner or later, our circumstances will change.

Escaping patterns

We seldom escape negative patterns just by changing our external circumstances. An internal shift must occur.

- Making more money alone won't enable us to overcome a scarcity mindset.
- Becoming a top performer won't automatically stop us feeling inadequate.
- Being in a relationship won't always cure our loneliness.
- Moving to a different country won't necessarily make our issues go away.

Seeking more of what we think we lack or need merely feeds the original pattern. We cannot feel prosperous, good enough or loved unless we change the way we think of ourselves.

We must look within.

We are the common denominators

If we keep failing at various projects, business ideas or relationships, the common denominator is us. When the same negative patterns keep repeating in our life, the issue is often us. We're getting in our own way.

If so, we might need to look more closely at that common denominator and make the necessary changes.

Our problems follow us

We cannot run away from our problems. Moving to a new place may enable us to gain experiences and discover new perspectives, but if the same issues arise over and over, it usually means that *we* are the problem.

While we can escape our environment, we can't escape ourselves.

Wanting something for nothing

Lack of success is often the result of wanting something for nothing —of trying to avoid doing the hard work while hoping to get the results we desire.

For example, that's when we want to:

- Make money without offering valuable products or services,
- Lose weight without changing our lifestyle, or
- Gain muscle without exercising consistently.

When we want to get something for nothing and refuse to acknowledge consistent hard work as a basic fact of life, we will struggle.

Tackling the wrong problems

We tend to focus on the wrong problems to avoid having to solve our actual problems. Often, this means we focus on the outside world so that we don't have to look within. We focus on superficial issues and make cosmetic changes, so we don't have to make cosmic changes.

Let's look ourselves in the mirror and ask what problems we're avoiding?

Our life's trajectory only changes when we're willing to tackle real problems. And we usually know what these real problems are.

3

ON THE TANGIBLE VS. THE INTANGIBLE

Imagination is stronger than willpower

When performing stretching exercises, close your eyes and visualize yourself being more flexible. You'll notice that this helps relax your body and it enables you to increase your flexibility. Put differently, you can do with imagination what you cannot do with force alone.

The same goes for any of our goals. Our imagination is more powerful than our willpower. When we have a compelling vision, we feel more energized and start taking action to make it a reality. Imagination enables us to forget about the barriers in front of us and overcome our mental limitations.

Ultimately, imagination is what differentiates us from any other living creature. We can use it to envision an uncertain and frightening future. Or we can use it to get excited about our goals.

Imagination is our superpower. Let's make sure it works for us, not against us.

The invisible is more powerful than the visible

We often try to change what is outside of us. The problem is that the visible is a manifestation of the invisible. What we can see—whether it is a physical product or something more intangible such as a political system or society as a whole—started as ideas in people's mind. These ideas were acted upon and came into existence. In other words, the visible world is the result of invisible forces.

If true, whatever change we want to bring must start in the realm of the invisible. Trying to change the visible is like attempting to change the shadows on a wall rather than what's creating them.

At the core of societal changes is a battle of ideas in people's minds. And at the core of individual change is a control over one's own mind. Therefore, to create change, we must affect change in one's mind and/or in other people's minds.

Ultimately, most of our suffering comes from the misconception that the tangible world (what's happening outside of us) is more real or more important than the intangible world (what's happening inside of us).

The power of subjective reality

The more we focus on what we can control, the more we can change ourselves *and* the world. This is the paradox of subjective reality. Focusing on the inside (the subjective) enables us to impact the world outside (the objective).

Everything is interconnected

It's easy to feel powerless. It's difficult to understand how we can impact the political system, the economy or the fate of our nation. While our individual power may be limited, it isn't insignificant. We often perceive society as an entity that is outside of us. We see the government or our country as something abstract. However, society, the government, countries, companies or every other institution is, first and foremost, made of people. We are a tiny part of society or government. We constitute a small fraction of our nation or the company we work for.

As such, our actions matter. With our behavior, we influence other people all day long. In each of our interactions, we project who we are and how we want the world to be. Therefore, let's notice when we try to remove ourselves from the equation and blame the system. Then, let's ask ourselves what we can do to make change, no matter how insignificant it may seem. Ultimately, our actions impact others and can bring positive change.

We may not change the world, but we can change something.

Worshipping the tangible

We often give too much importance to the tangible while we neglect the intangible. Yet the most important things are intangible, whether it be happiness, health, love, gratitude, friendship, creativity, wisdom or a sense of meaning. When we forget that simple fact and worship the tangible, we lose track of what matters most.

Unconditional giving

There is no true giving when we seek to receive something in return. Let's avoid:

- Helping someone hoping they will help us in return. That's being insincere.
- Doing small favors for others so that they will owe us one. That's being manipulative.
- Giving a compliment to someone before making a request. That's being dishonest.

True unconditional giving can only exist when we give without expecting anything in return—not now, and not in the future.

Transactional giving

When we give with the hope of receiving, we turn each interaction into a transaction (i.e. I scratch your back, you scratch mine).

We can switch from transactional giving to unconditional giving by seeing the act of giving as an interaction between us and the whole universe. Unconditional giving results from the inner belief that, if we help people around us whenever we can, without sacrificing our needs, we'll receive support from the universe.

In a nutshell, true giving only exists when we expect nothing in return. If not, we're just transacting with people, or we're manipulating them in the hope of personal gain, either now or in the future.

THOUGHTS

Thoughts are both a blessing and a curse.

They can enable us to create the life we desire.

Or they can wreak havoc in our lives and in the lives of people around us.

Let's pay attention to our thoughts.

4

ON VALUES

Our values are what stays with us when everything else is gone. It's the backbone that makes us who we are.

When we compromise our values for money, fame, power or success, we begin to lose ourselves. The first crack in our psyche appears when we start saying things such as, "but everybody else is doing it" or, "it's just one time".

The point of having values is to stand by them regardless of what everyone else is doing. Values act as pillars that orient our decisions. They are what enables us to broadcast what we want the world to be. In the absence of values such as courage, integrity, humility or compassion, the state of the world slowly begins to erode. In the absence of values, we become powerless.

The cost of values

Values aren't a way to boost our ego or to signal to others how virtuous we are. Values are costly. They have real consequences in the real world. For instance:

- Refusing to behave in a way that we deem unethical may cost us money (at least in the short term).

- Having the courage to speak up may cost us our careers and, in some cases, much more.
- Being honest and telling the truth may lead us to be hated by many people.

When we have strong values, we have skin in the game.

It will cost us something.

That's how we know we're serious.

Speaking up vs. staying quiet

In an ideal world, we would speak up every time we see something wrong with society. But if we speak too much or in the wrong way, or on certain topics, we can get in trouble. For instance, in authoritarian regimes, we may end up in jail, or worse, dead. In more democratic regimes, we may jeopardize our careers, be ostracized, or even "canceled".

There is always a trade-off.

How much good for society will we be able to do if we are silenced, incarcerated or dead?

But if we stay too quiet, nothing will change. If we tolerate too much abuse, corruption or violation of our rights, our country may slowly turn into an authoritarian regime.

How much should we speak up and in what way? And when should we keep a low profile and operate in the shadows?

There is no clear answer. It's always a balancing act.

5

ON MORALITY

Does the end justify the means?

Is it okay to steal, lie, cheat or manipulate people to achieve a "noble" goal?

Should I be willing to do anything to sell you this book because I believe it could change your life?

The problem with that line of thinking is that it assumes we know what's best for people. It assumes that we're the enlightened ones and they are the ones who need to be enlightened by us. We may be right. Our product, service or knowledge may be invaluable, but this is a slippery slope. When we believe the end justifies the means, we may start lying to sell our product, service or ideas. Soon, small lies turn into big ones. We become more and more egotistical. And, over time, we may feel the need to tell others what they should eat, wear, talk about and, ultimately, think.

In truth, we understand the world far less than we think. We fail to grasp its complexity and fall for countless biases. As a result, while we may believe we know what's best for ourselves and others, we're likely wrong. Hitler, Stalin and Mao were convinced they knew the best way to organize society. It's fair to say that millions of people very strongly disagreed (and still disagree) with their ideologies.

At a more fundamental level, what gives us the right to tell others how they should live their lives? People are free not to want our product, service or advice. They are entitled to hate our ideas. They have the right not to want to support our vision. We're not the center of the universe. People aren't pawns we can use to reach "noble" goals.

No. The end probably doesn't justify the means.

But everybody is doing it

Acting the same as everybody else is a sure way to tolerate questionable behavior in ourselves and in others, and become a poor role model.

We do things because we believe they are the right things to do. However, just because others are doing something doesn't give us permission to do the same thing. If we behave that way, we are merely mimicking others instead of thinking for ourselves.

Everybody might be doing it.

But it doesn't mean *we* should.

Karma (or the absence of it)

We often believe that bad people will eventually pay for the harm they do to others and society.

But is this true?

- Con artists can be around for decades, going from one scam to the next.
- Corrupt politicians can have "brilliant" careers with just a few hiccups along the way.
- Dictators sometimes live to a ripe old age, never being judged, let alone going to jail.

Yes, people often end up being caught. But not always. While they may not be punished by society, their punishment is leading an unhappy and tormented life—or so the argument goes. For some people, maybe. But not for all. The point is, believing that bad people will pay for their crime is a coping mechanism. It's what we want to believe. In truth, there are people who take advantage of others and cause harm to society. And oftentimes, these people will never be caught.

Fake arguments

He's jealous.

He's just a hater.

People don't like rich people.

Influencers, celebrities or gurus often use these arguments whenever they're criticized. Instead of responding to fair criticism, they deflect them by using blanket statements and by gaslighting "naysayers".

But not everyone is a hater or is jealous of "successful" people. Often, people just don't like scam artists stealing money from people who have little to begin with.

Having money isn't a free pass to behaving badly. On the contrary, wealthy people should be held to higher standards and called out whenever they engage in shady practices. There is nothing wrong with being wealthy, but there is everything wrong with being a wealthy scumbag.

For instance, celebrities who have endorsed shady businesses may well say they didn't know. But, in the end, they gave these "businesses" a bigger platform and pocketed the money while actively leading thousands of people to lose their money. In other words, they grew richer while others grew poorer all the while pretending to be on their side.

When you're living in abject poverty, scamming people to survive might be understandable. But when you're rich, what excuse can you have?

Getting away with anything

Politicians can be involved in numerous scandals but still be elected to prominent positions.

Notorious scammers can get out of jail just to engage in yet another shady business after their release.

Influencers can scam their audience repeatedly with crypto "investments" and other dubious projects and can still make millions.

What do all these examples say about what we value as a society?

When the threshold for ethics is low—and when people are overly forgiving of wrongdoers—no one has any incentive to be held to a higher standard.

Why would they, when others seem to be getting away with so much?

6

ON HAPPINESS

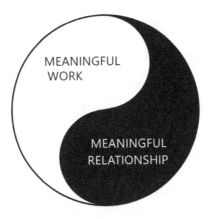

The simple formula for happiness

Most of our time is spent at work and/or interacting with other people. Every time I reflect on what makes for a fulfilling life, this simple formula comes to mind:

Meaningful work + meaningful relationships.

If we have none of them, we'll be miserable.

If we have one of them, we'll be living.

But if we manage to have both, we'll be thriving.

The root of unhappiness

We don't need a lot to be happy, but we want to be happier than our neighbor.

That's where our problems begin.

Happiness and social media

The internet, especially social media, distorts reality and creates insecurities. People show their best selves online, which leads to unrealistic standards in terms of beauty, health, wealth or happiness.

It might be reasonable to say that our emotional well-being is inversely proportionate to the amount of time we spend scrolling on social media.

Finding ourselves in the era of social media

When we fill our time with endless scrolling and swiping, we rob ourselves of quiet time we could use to reflect on our life.

To discover ourselves and uncover our gifts, talents and purpose, we must spend time both alone and with others. By being alone, we can process the information we're exposed to during the day, and we can reflect on what we've learned through our interactions with others. In short, being alone provides us with the space needed to cultivate our intuition and our sense of self.

The problem is that time spent on social media is not really time spent alone; and it's not really time spent with others either.

Social media as fiction

Being on social media is like reading fiction. It can be entertaining, but it's not the real world. The issue arises when we aspire to live the same life as the fictional characters portrayed in it.

More specifically, social media extrapolates our human tendencies.

- Our desire to do a little better in life is replaced with a desire to become a millionaire, buy luxury items, develop a six-pack or look twenty years younger than our age.
- Our desire to be content is replaced with a need to be as happy as, or happier than, the way others portray themselves on social media. This usually entails having a lavish lifestyle, making a lot of money, being in better shape and so on.
- Our desire to be loved by a few people around us (as it used to be) is replaced with our desire to be loved by countless people around the world.

Add to the mix a bunch of ads that play on our insecurities and it's no wonder many of us feel inadequate. The overall message we receive is simple:

We are not good enough.

Made-up problems

Many of our so-called problems are given to us by society or people around us. Influencers on social media make us feel as though we aren't good, smart, beautiful or successful enough. And commercials "remind" us of our inadequacies while trying to sell us the solution to our "problems".

Perhaps the solution to many of our "problems" is to take a break from TV and social media, and grab a coffee or tea with a friend. Or perhaps it is to go for a walk, draw or complete a puzzle.

Could it really be that simple?

The trap of comparison

Let's not judge people, because they fight inner battles we have no idea about.

Let's not envy people, because what they project on the outside might be the opposite of what they feel inside.

When we compare ourselves to the way others portray themselves, we distort reality and suffer. We must accept that others have their own issues to deal with—and so do we. We must respect both their inner battles and our own.

All we can do is walk our unique path with dignity and self-compassion while celebrating our progress.

Our true wealth

Our ability to maintain a positive emotional state most of the time enables us to enjoy life. Anyone who has ever been depressed, or at least deeply sad, knows how challenging this is. When we are feeling bad, everything looks dull. We lack the motivation to do anything, and life appears meaningless. Conversely, when we feel good, we have more energy to pursue exciting projects and can make the most of our lives.

Our emotional health is our true wealth.

OUR FIRST THOUGHT IN THE MORNING

The first thought that pops into our mind as we wake up matters more than we think.

Let's observe it.

Then, let's make sure it's one of gratitude.

Being grateful for the small things

Our level of fulfilment is inversely correlated to the size of the things we appreciate in our life. The more we appreciate the smaller things, the happier and more blessed we'll feel. For this reason, continuously seeking bigger successes often fails to bring us the happiness we hoped for.

If we can't appreciate smaller things, we are unlikely to appreciate bigger ones.

Appreciating before it's too late

Money seems unimportant until we run out of it and can't pay the bills.

We're not concerned about oxygen until a wave catches us by surprise and we're underwater, desperately trying to breathe.

We don't worry about our health until we become ill.

Sadly, we struggle to appreciate what we have. We take our family and friends for granted, we disrespect our body by indulging in fast food and alcohol, and we complain about our jobs.

Having a fulfilling life is mostly about learning to want what we already have. It's being grateful for all the things we're blessed with.

What we appreciate, appreciates. What we're grateful for makes our glass look fuller.

Abundance and gratitude

Abundance starts with gratitude. Nothing will ever be enough if we can't appreciate what we already have; simply because scarcity is a pattern. We must change the pattern, not merely the external circumstances.

Entitlement and gratitude

Entitlement is the opposite of gratitude. It's when we believe we're owed something for no reason. Meanwhile, gratitude is when we learn to appreciate the gifts we were given, whether we "deserve" them or not.

We can't feel both entitled and grateful.

We must choose one.

LOVE, FORGIVE, APPRECIATE, APOLOGIZE

Love.

Forgive others.

Show your appreciation.

Apologize when you make a mistake.

Keep these four things in mind each day.

Choosing our state of mind

When we listen to a motivational speaker, we may feel a surge of motivation.

When we read a spiritual book, we may feel more present and more appreciative.

When we watch a video on slow living, we may feel the need to be less ambitious and spend time to smell the roses a little more.

And when we're talking with a negative friend, we may feel demotivated and uninspired.

The information we're exposed to deeply affects our mood. Therefore, we must decide what kind of mood is most likely to help us live a fulfilling life. Then, we must select the information most conducive to that mood and discard the rest.

The point is this. Our state of mind matters. Let's choose it based on what we want to accomplish and how we want to live our lives. And let's remember what we need right now is not necessarily what others need or what's popular.

Drama vs. peace of mind

Some people live a drama-filled life while others enjoy a peaceful life. Coincidence? Not necessarily.

People who desire to live a peaceful life choose peace over petty issues, needless worries and unnecessary conflicts.

Meanwhile, people whose life is full of drama tend to value being right over being peaceful. They seek to protect their pride at all costs. And when they find themselves in a peaceful situation, they feel uneasy. Soon enough, they'll find a way to bring dramas back because that's what they know and what seems familiar to them. We often reproduce the patterns we are the most familiar with, whether those patterns are working for or against us.

Feeling at peace most of the time is attainable, but we must want to feel that way. We can't be at peace if we want to be superior to others, desire to live a fast-paced life, seek high status or worship material success. When we do so, we enter the comparison game. Peace of mind exists outside of any comparison. If we desire peace, we must seek it as earnestly as we can. And if we don't want it, we must admit it to ourselves.

Be miserable or be happy

In life, we can focus on:

- What we don't have,
- What we don't like about ourselves,
- What might go wrong,
- Our past mistakes,
- Our failures,
- Our problems, and,
- All the people who wronged us or hurt us.

Or we can focus on:

- What we have,
- What we like about ourselves,
- What might go well,
- Our accomplishments,
- Our past successes,
- All the opportunities in our life, and
- All the people who support us or care about us.

What we choose to focus on will largely dictate how we feel.

We can be miserable.

Or we can be happy.

THE OBSTACLES TO OUR HAPPINESS

We'd rather be right than be happy.

We choose success over happiness.

We want to be happier than our neighbor.

We focus on what we lack rather than on what we have.

Pain vs. pleasure

Meaning often requires pain. Yet, most of us want to experience pleasure while avoiding pain.

But is that possible or even desirable? Can anything exist without its opposite? Can too much pleasure become the end of pleasure?

- If we go to our favorite restaurant every day, the pleasure we get from that activity will likely dissipate.
- If we travel all year round, the joy of travelling might start to fade.
- If we have no struggles, the fulfilment we get from overcoming challenges will disappear.

A meaningful life requires a healthy amount of pain and challenge. Fulfilment results from overcoming challenges and testing our limits, at least occasionally.

Often, too much pleasure doesn't lead to the level of fulfilment we're seeking.

Choosing our pain

For the most part, we can choose the kind of pain we want to experience in life. In fact, the more we choose our pain and challenges, the more we may be able to protect ourselves against unwanted pain.

For instance, self-discipline isn't pleasant, but it can prevent many problems down the road. Doing challenging workouts a few times a week may be uncomfortable, but it may improve our overall health. And completing a difficult project may be mentally taxing but it will enable us to introduce "useful" pain that will make us feel more alive.

Whenever possible, we should probably choose our pain. This will make us more resilient to future painful events that we may have little control over.

Respecting our issues

We shouldn't deny ourselves the right to feel a certain way due to personal issues, even when these issues may seem insignificant. It's not a competition. There is no pride in having more or bigger issues than others, and there is no shame or guilt in having fewer or smaller issues either.

By accepting our problems and facing them, we increase our contribution to the world. In doing so, we acquire more wisdom, learn to love ourselves more and feel better as a result. Being depressed, sad, guilty or ashamed of ourselves is seldom the optimal way to improve our life and the lives of people around us.

Respecting people's issues

Let's respect other people's problems no matter how small or insignificant they may seem to us. They have the right to have their own problems too—and should be allowed to deal with them and grow through the process.

Never-ending guilt

We always seem to feel guilty or ashamed about something.

When we do well financially, we feel guilty knowing that many people around the world aren't. When we enjoy free time with our family, we may feel guilty for not helping more people—taking on more patients, dedicating more time to charity work or helping our colleagues. When we spend too much time at work, we can feel guilty for not spending enough time with our family.

Perhaps we should give ourselves permission not to feel guilty all the time.

Jealousy

Jealousy is a sign that we're trying to step into another person's shoes. Let's stay in *our* shoes. Let's have the courage to live *our* life rather than trying to live someone else's. That's how we'll discover our unique path and make the most of our talents and skills.

The secret to solving problems

The best way to solve problems is to avoid them in the first place.

The second best way is to reframe them as challenges or opportunities and/or to deal with them.

For instance:

You can solve the problem of tooth cavities by:

- Brushing your teeth regularly and having regular check-ups (best way).
- Perceiving it as an opportunity to respect yourself more by visiting the dentist more regularly (second best way).
- Seeing a dentist as soon as possible (third best way).

You can solve the problem of debt by:

- Refusing to get into debt in the first place (best way).
- Seeing debt as an opportunity to find ways to make more money and upgrade your skills (second best way).
- Doing whatever you can to pay off your debt (third best way).

You can solve the problem of lies and deception by:

- Being as honest as possible in every situation (best way).
- looking within yourself to figure out why you need to lie (second best way).
- Saying the truth and apologizing to people you lied to (third best way).

The point is, the same way we want to prevent diseases from happening years in advance, we should strive to prevent problems from happening long before they occur.

Preventing problems

Below are a few recommendations that may prevent many problems from happening:

- Don't smoke.
- Drink alcohol moderately (or not at all).
- Exercise regularly.
- Eat healthily.
- Avoid debt.
- Diversify your investments.
- Avoid doing anything that doesn't feel right to you.
- Don't rush into any major decisions.
- Deal with any issue quickly.
- Don't let things escalate.
- Get insurance where needed.
- Avoid unnecessary risks.

Many problems are avoidable but it's hard for us to notice. After all, we can't know about things that haven't happened yet. For instance, we won't hear in the news about an accident that didn't occur when a drunk person chose to order a cab instead of driving themselves home.

That's why the case for prevention is harder to make and why people tend to let problems occur through negligence, or lack of preparedness.

Whenever possible, strive to prevent problems from happening in the first place.

Pessimism as a coping mechanism

People often use pessimism to avoid responsibilities. They'd rather see themselves as hopeless victims than perform the hard work required to change their attitude or situation. Sadly, in doing so, they severely limit their growth and rob themselves of their incredible ability to change.

Pessimism vs. realism

In many ways, what we expect and desire can often become our reality. A group of people with a shared vision and positive expectations can achieve wonderful things, but the opposite is also true. A group of people with no vision and no hope for the future won't be able to improve their situation.

At a subconscious level, pessimists see the world as fixed and immutable. Nothing they can do matters. On the other hand, realists see the world as it is, but understand they can make it a little better with the right mindset and a lot of effort. To know whether we're a pessimist or a realist, we can ask ourselves the following question:

Am I secretly hoping that things will turn out the way I predicted (i.e., badly) so that I can feel right and tell others, "I told you so"?

Our negativity bias

Our brain is designed to notice any potential threat so that we can act quickly to protect ourselves. This is why fear sells. News doesn't report on everything that is going well in the world. Instead, it reports on deadly wars, diseases, murders, economic crises and other issues that may threaten us.

To counterbalance our natural tendency toward negativity, we should focus more time on what's good in our life and in the world. This is not delusion or blind optimism, it's merely an attempt to overcome our natural negativity bias.

Feeling dead inside

What our brain perceives as new experiences decreases significantly over time. Babies and the elderly see the world differently. When we're young, there are a lot of firsts. Our first kiss. Our first job. Our first trip abroad. Our first sushi. Our first speech. Our first driving lesson. But this doesn't happen so often as we age. As time passes, our brain runs increasingly on autopilot. What was once new and exciting has become old and dull.

Perhaps the antidote to a lack of "aliveness" is to remain perpetually curious about how the world works while challenging ourselves and trying new things.

We're not necessarily old, we just feel old.

EVERY DAY SHOULD BE CHERISHED

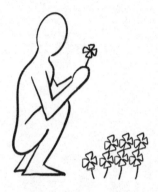

We miss the day in front of us because we want to be somewhere else.

We worry about the past or look forward to the future. In each case, we aren't *here*.

Every day can be cherished—but only if we practice treating it as such.

7

ON SELF-WORTH

Our sense of self

Our sense of self is who we believe ourselves to be and how we think we must behave to protect that "self".

But it is ever-changing. As we gain experience, we evolve and the world around us changes too. It means that there is always tension between who we thought ourselves to be and who we are becoming. There is an inner battle between the urge to maintain the status quo and the willingness to change.

Life will demand that we update our sense of self—that we change our "identity" over time. Let's welcome that truth and be open to change.

What is our self-worth based on?

We all worship something. That is, we all give a disproportionate amount of time and attention to one or more things. And what we worship often determines what we base our sense of self-worth on. For example:

- Some people equate success with wealth. If they fail to land a lucrative career or build a thriving business, they see themselves as failures.
- Other people seek attention. When they fail to become famous or aren't appreciated enough, they feel bad about themselves.
- Others are perfectionists. If they host dinner and fail to cook the "perfect" meal, they think of themselves as failures.

Put differently, we all base our sense of self-worth on something—and usually multiple things. It's not necessarily a problem, though. But it might be a good idea to observe what we base our self-worth on and see whether it's healthy.

Let's not be ashamed of what we're currently worshipping. The first step is awareness. By observing ourselves without judgment, we can start making the necessary adjustments in our lives.

The voices in our head

Who do we listen to, try to prove wrong or hope to please? Who is occupying real estate in our mind without our permission? Is it our parents? Colleagues? Boss? Teachers? Ex partner?

We all have many voices in our head. They define us and confine us —often without our consent. To free ourselves, we must start letting go of these voices. It begins by paying attention to our internal dialogue.

Being somebody vs. being nobody

We try hard to become somebody, but perhaps we should aim at becoming nobody.

Seeking to be somebody means:

- Competing with others,
- Obsessing over the results,
- Attempting to see ourselves as better than others, and
- Thinking of ourselves as self-contained.

Meanwhile, being nobody means:

- Doing what we feel drawn toward without comparing ourselves to others,
- Seeing others as our equals,
- Deriving pleasure from the process rather than seeking the outcome, and
- Asking for help rather than thinking of ourselves as self-contained.

Put differently, trying to be somebody means thinking of ourselves as special (i.e., better than others), while trying to be nobody means thinking of ourselves as unique (i.e., different from others).

When we see ourselves as special, we try to be better than others, which creates never-ending suffering and a constant desire to prove ourselves to the world. It leads us to believe we shouldn't depend on others as it would make us appear weak (and inferior to them).

When we see ourselves as unique, we let go of the comparison game as we recognize its inherent flaws. We realize that we only need to fight our own battles. The best thing we can do is to accept our uniqueness, be kind to ourselves and rejoice in any small improvement we make while facing our challenges.

We don't have to be special. We must simply embrace our uniqueness.

The benefits of not feeling good enough

Not feeling good enough is often a sign that we want more out of life. We want to hold ourselves to a higher standard. Isn't that a sign of self-respect? Shouldn't we see it as a genuine desire to make good use of our talents and gifts?

If so, perhaps not feeling good enough isn't a bug, but a feature. As we welcome feelings of inadequacy and see them as part of the human experience, they begin to lose their power and fade away.

Adding to ourselves vs. expressing ourselves

Our desire to improve ourselves shouldn't make us feel as though we need to do more so that we can feel good enough and finally be accepted by others. A better way to see personal growth is as a tool to help us become more of who (we know) we already are deep down. How? By removing fears, insecurities and any other obstacles that prevent us from doing so. By unlearning and letting go of who we think we are so that we can live more authentically.

In short, personal growth is a process of elimination, not one of addition. By letting go of layers of fear, misconception and conditioning we can become our more authentic self.

Personal growth is amplifying who we are, not becoming someone else.

Self-acceptance vs. self-improvement

Self-improvement is important but so is self-acceptance. A relentless desire to improve ourselves often hides the inability to love ourselves as we are.

But how can we love ourselves as we are and improve ourselves at the same time?

This is a difficult question to answer.

The answer might be a healthy dose of gratitude, humility and self-compassion.

- Gratitude so that we appreciate our life the way it is right now.
- Humility so that we understand that we are merely normal people.
- Self-compassion so that we accept our flaws, failures and mistakes as an inherent part of being human.

With these three allies, we can start growing without feeling the need to criticize ourselves all the time.

Walking the path

By trying to be loved by everybody, we are loved by nobody.

By doing what everyone else is doing, we end up living someone else's life.

We have a unique path to walk.

Let's walk it, at our own pace, in our own time, without comparing ourselves with others.

Addictions and emotions

Many of us struggle with food, drug or alcohol addiction. Or we continuously seek people's attention and validation. The solution is simple: we should eat less, refrain from consuming drugs and alcohol and stop looking for people's approval.

Or is it?

The main reason we suffer from these addictions in the first place is often because we are somewhat dissatisfied. For instance, if we spend most of our day at what we consider a meaningless job, how can our frustration not manifest in other areas of our lives? People who have indulged in comfort food after a stressful day understand how frustration may impact their lives negatively.

In the end, most of our problems are emotional issues that stem from lack of motivation, poor self-awareness, feelings of worthlessness or fears of various kinds.

Knowing what we should do is seldom the real issue. Most of us know that we shouldn't smoke, drink alcohol, eat junk food or take drugs. We know that we should probably exercise more. We also know that we should go to bed earlier. But knowing what to do is of little value if we can't motivate ourselves to do it.

"Firing" people in your life

Let go of people who disrespect you.

Part ways with customers who cause you headaches.

Ignore naysayers who criticize you unfairly or relentlessly.

Fire influencers, Youtubers or writers who don't make your life better.

Stop watching news that plays on your fears.

You don't have to tolerate people who don't respect you. You don't have to be around people who aren't rooting for you.

Fire people and regain your peace of mind.

8

ON COMPASSION

Distance and harm

It's easier to harm someone who is thousands of miles away than someone sitting next to us. It's easier to harm someone we see as different—different country, religion, ethnicity, cultural background —than someone we see as just like us. We need to perceive people as different from us or make them invisible so that harming them becomes more acceptable. For instance:

- Dropping a bomb on a city is easier than killing each person ourselves while looking them in the eye.
- Harassing someone online is easier than bullying them in person.
- It is easier to gossip behind someone's back than to tell them what we think about them face-to-face.

In summary, harming others requires distance whether emotionally or physically. We don't want to harm people we know or who appear like us. Sadly, by creating distance and by avoiding putting ourselves in other people's shoes, we can do more harm than we would ever imagine.

Distance and caring

The greater the distance, the less emotionally affected we are, and the more we can tolerate the intolerable.

For instance, the more intermediaries a company has, the easier it is for them to close their eyes to what's happening outside of their facilities. They might feel responsible for what's going on in their stores, but not in suppliers' factories thousands of miles away.

In short, the less we see, the more we can tolerate.

Creating physical or emotional distance often enables us to make more inhumane decisions. A president of a country that declares a war won't be the one sent to the frontline. The CEO firing thousands of employees won't be the one losing his job. Distance helps them make such decisions.

At the same time, difficult decisions are often necessary. And the more we remove ourselves from the day-to-day operations, the easier it becomes to make tough decisions. If so, perhaps creating distance is a necessary evil for any society to function properly. But it may lead us to lack empathy and make decisions that bring pain and suffering to many.

Macro-level vs. micro-level compassion

Caring for the fate of humanity and caring for people on an individual level may appear incompatible. In other words, when we care for the well-being of humanity, it becomes difficult to care deeply for each person individually. Perhaps this is because we must be somewhat inconsiderate and distant if we wish to keep the big picture in mind. Perhaps this is because we must make difficult decisions that will affect some individuals negatively.

This is one of the dilemmas of having more responsibility. If we hope to improve the lives of millions of people, we must be pragmatic and sometimes, perhaps even ruthless. This may be what prevents us from connecting with people at a deeper level and acting with compassion. One alternative is to try to please everybody. But if we do so, we won't be able to make any decisions for the good of the community as there will always be someone hurt by our decisions.

Here is an extreme example:

Let's say we must choose between one of these two options:

- Killing one person to save ten, or
- Doing nothing and letting ten people die.

How can we act from a place of deep compassion while killing one person? On the other hand, how can we be so heartless as to let ten people die when we could save them by sacrificing only one? This is the paradox of compassion. It raises the fundamental question:

What is compassion?

Perhaps we should differentiate between two types of compassion:

- Macro-level compassion. caring for society, and
- Micro-level compassion. caring for specific individuals.

Now, the way to reconcile them or navigate between one and the other effectively might be an impossible task.

Misguided compassion

We often behave differently when in the presence of someone who is disabled. But it seems to me that, before deciding how to act, we should try to see things from their perspective.

People want to be treated as people. When we see their differences or disabilities first before seeing anything else, we disrespect them. When, out of "compassion", we are overly kind, give them too much slack or assume they can't perform tasks and do it for them, we prevent them from having the human experience they're looking for. In other words, we take away their dignity as humans.

I call this misguided compassion.

Compassion and experience

It's easier to be compassionate toward others when we have gone through similar challenges ourselves. We can put ourselves in others' shoes more readily. But when they're going through something that is alien to us, we risk seeing them as complacent or undisciplined. Generally speaking, this is why the more experience we accumulate, the more compassionate we become.

9

ON MEANING AND PURPOSE

The meaning of life is to live in alignment with who we believe ourselves to be. This requires:

- Knowing who we are, and
- Having the courage to make our own choices and follow our unique path.

Finding meaning

If we can't find meaning in our life, let's create it. Let's set a meaningful goal. Let's craft an inspiring vision. As we're busy infusing our life with meaning, the meaning of life may reveal itself. And if it doesn't, we can just keep creating meaning in our life.

A movie worth watching

Is our life a movie worth watching? What quest are we embarking on? What fears are we facing? What challenges are we tackling?

Life is about overcoming our challenges and expressing ourselves. We are on a hero's journey. When we embrace our personal quest, we make our life an interesting movie. When we run away from our challenges, hide, procrastinate or numb ourselves, we create a lousy movie.

Life becomes meaningful when we embrace our challenges and seek to express ourselves to the best of our abilities—at least, that's how it seems to me.

Problems vs. opportunities

Each problem we face is an opportunity to reflect on the meaning of our life and the direction we want it to take. It's also an opportunity for us to decide what kind of person we aspire to be. In the same way a hero in a movie is defined by the choices they make when facing difficulties, our life is defined by the choices we make when facing challenges.

Searching for immortality

Perhaps the measure of a good life is what's left after we are gone— the people we touched, the children we raised, the work we did in our community, the inventions we helped to create.

Living a good life might mean leaving a part of us behind, somewhere in the world. It might be an attempt to do the impossible: reaching immortality.

When less is better

More options can be a blessing, but it can also be a curse. When we have unlimited options, we can be at a loss. We don't know where to start or what to do. We struggle to find meaning. What goal should we pursue? Where should we live? What project should we focus our time on?

But when we have fewer options due to a lack of time, resources, and/or disabilities, the path ahead often becomes more straightforward. Sometimes, having fewer options is better. It forces us to commit to one path, go deeper with it and live a more meaningful life.

Sometimes, having fewer choices is simply better.

The seasons of life

There are different seasons during our life, but also over a decade, a year, a month and even a day.

Life requires us to embrace the push and pull dynamic to experience it to the fullest and obtain many of the results we aspire to. That is, sometimes, we need to "hustle" and get things done (push). Other times, we need to step away from our problems and let our subconscious work on it (pull). Sometimes, we need to be highly logical and focused (push). Other times we need to zoom out, trust the universe and abandon our need for control—at least temporarily (pull).

When we rely on force only, we experience unnecessary struggle and tension, and, often, achieve subpar results. Below are the different seasons we might want to pay attention to:

- **Planting seasons:** we plant the seeds of our successes by setting intentions, writing down goals and creating plans.
- **Watering seasons:** we put our head down and work toward our goals with focus and consistency.
- **Reaping seasons:** we acknowledge our wins and reward ourselves.
- **Resting seasons:** we take a step back, relax and let our subconscious work in the background.

Seasons in a day:

- Setting goals and intentions in the morning or the night before (planting).
- Working on our major tasks with limited distractions (watering).
- Acknowledging our small and big wins at the end of the day (reaping).
- Going for a walk, working out, meditating or relaxing in the evening (resting).

Seasons in a month:

- Setting goals and intentions at the beginning of the month (planting).
- Working on our major goals every day (watering).
- Reviewing our goals and acknowledging our small and big wins at the end of the month (reaping).
- Relaxing during the weekends, going on short trips, hiking, meeting with our friends (resting).

Similarly, there are seasons in a year. We can:

- Set goals in January (planting).
- Work on them daily (watering).
- Acknowledge our wins in December (reaping).
- Take breaks every 90 days (resting).

Plant, water, reap and rest.

Let's repeat the cycle and find our own rhythm. When we're pushing too hard, let's stop. When we're not doing enough, let's push a little bit more.

A blueprint for life

In your twenties, use your energy to experiment. Try new things, explore the world, find out what you like and what you're good at.

In your thirties, use your energy to reach mastery. Build on your strengths and get to a position where you can do meaningful work you enjoy.

In your forties, use your energy, skill and knowledge strategically to free your time. Scale down. Or scale up by leveraging other people's time. Care less about what people think, integrate past experiences and be more nuanced.

In your fifties and beyond, teach, advise and mentor others. Use your knowledge and wisdom to contribute to society in a meaningful and enjoyable way for you.

Why do anything?

Why do something rather than nothing? Why strive for anything at all?

Inside each of us, there is a part driven by ego. We want to acquire status so that we can be respected, provide for our family and leave offspring. We also want to express our creativity, find a meaningful cause to fight for or experience pleasant feelings.

So why do anything at all?

Perhaps because we must hang out on earth for a while. Therefore, we might as well experience all kinds of things, learn various lessons and even understand a little bit more about how the universe works.

What else are we supposed to do?

Growing old

We can lament about getting old or we can realize that millions of people didn't or won't make it to our age. Many people born the exact same day as us are already gone. Upon that realization, we must appreciate the blessing of being granted yet another day on this planet.

Growing older is a blessing many people didn't get a chance to experience; it's not a curse. Why be envious of younger people when we have already lived the years they haven't yet—and that some of them never will?

Acting old

When we behave as though we're old, we signal our body that we're ready to leave soon. As a result, we age faster. Conversely, when we realize that we can't retire from life, we remain active and keep pursuing exciting projects. As a result, we will age more gracefully. At least, that's my theory.

Let's make sure we have clear, exciting plans and a strong desire to stick around. Our body will likely try to support us the best it can.

Life as a process of elimination

As we age, we learn to let go of everything unimportant and focus on what is important. The biggest challenge might be to realize what matters most to us as early as possible.

Put differently, life is a game in which we keep pursuing what we think we want until we realize that it's not what is really important. Our interaction with the external world acts as a feedback mechanism. By interacting with our environment, we discover what we like and don't like, what we're good at and poor at, and begin to figure out who we are in the process.

Perhaps eliminating what doesn't matter is how we make our life more meaningful.

Noise vs. signal

Most of the information we consume each day is somewhat useless, if not harmful. It won't matter tomorrow, next week or next year, and it won't make us any better or any more knowledgeable. In other words, it's noise. As information flows faster and in an ever-greater volume, the ratio of noise to signal increases. As a result, what matters becomes lost in a sea of irrelevant and pointless information.

One of our main goals and biggest challenges in life is to reduce noise and increase signal. That's how we extract more meaning out of our lives and move closer to our vision.

ONE RULE FOR LIFE

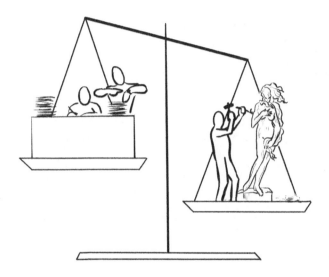

Do more of what makes you feel proud of yourself.

Do less of what doesn't.

At the end of our lives

"I wish I'd bought more stuff." "I regret not having watched more movies." "If only I could have spent more time on social media."

We won't say any of these things on our deathbed.

Instead, we'll reflect on the quality of our relationships, whether we expressed our feelings authentically or had the courage to pursue the endeavors that mattered to us.

Similarly, at our funerals, nobody will say:

"They had a wonderful house, beautiful cars, nice clothes and millions of dollars in the bank."

People will talk about who we were as a person, not what we had.

If so, to live a fulfilling life, we must focus on creating rather than on consuming, on being rather than having and on expressing ourselves rather than seeking something outside of us to fill a void within.

Realizing vs. chasing

There are things we realize from within and things we chase outside of us. For instance: mastery, curiosity, compassion, meaning or passion are inner realizations.

- *Mastery* is when we realize we want to become better.
- *Curiosity* is when we feel the desire to understand the world better.
- *(Self-)Compassion* is when we sense the need to be kinder to ourselves and to others.
- *Meaning* is when we feel the urge to pursue a meaningful endeavor.
- *Passion* is when we want to do things we're passionate about.

Meanwhile, things such as money, power or fame are external concepts we chase, often to fill a void within ourselves. As we learn more about ourselves, what we realize from within enables us to let go of our desire to chase what's without.

This is why what we realize internally is more powerful than what we chase externally.

Finding ourselves

To figure out what we're good at, what we love most and what gives meaning to our life, we must spend time alone reflecting.

But, if we spend too much time by ourselves, we risk missing out on the external perspectives we need to discover who we are. We learn about ourselves by interacting with people. We can identify our uniqueness by realizing how different we are from others. Our interaction with others enables us to receive feedback. What are people complimenting us on? What are we struggling with? What comes naturally to us? How are people acting and reacting in our presence? In a sense, people act as a mirror reflecting to us who we are. We need their help to figure ourselves out.

The point is, finding ourselves is a balancing act between spending time alone and interacting with others. Both activities give us feedback on who we are, what we want and what makes us unique.

We must spend time both alone *and* with others.

It's not for us

If we need to be told what to do, how to study or where to find the information, we're probably pursuing the wrong goals.

In truth, if we really want something, we will seek it. We will do whatever we can to make it a reality. We certainly won't wait for the answer to come to us, we will go find it. We'll figure out the best strategy. And we'll learn whatever is needed along the way.

If not, then it's probably not for us.

Selfishness and selflessness

Should we be selfish or selfless? And can we really be selfless?

People who think they are selfless, do what they do for a reason. Perhaps it makes them feel good. Perhaps they want to be admired or remembered for their selflessness. Or perhaps helping others is an attempt to overcome a feeling of unworthiness deep within. If so, we may argue that their actions are selfish, not selfless.

If everything we do is indeed somewhat selfish, perhaps we should find a way to help others *and* feel good about ourselves. In many aspects, that's how we are designed. But we tend to forget that and become obsessed with making money, seeking fame or trying to raise our status. In the process, we often lie, cheat and steal in the hope of feeling better and finally being good enough.

We are all selfish and want to feel good. If so, the solution might be to use our selfishness in a constructive way that both serves others and makes us feel good. This may help us live a more meaningful life.

The "key" to success

The right action for us can only be determined based on our current situation. And our situation is the result of the countless decisions we've made up until now. That's why generic advice can only take us so far. The context is missing—and our life story is not reflected.

The key to success lies in introspection. We are like a puzzle. The way we solve that puzzle is by unraveling new pieces over time through self-reflection. Using self-reflection, we can discover who we are, what we love to do, and what we're good at. It's how we figure out what works for us and what doesn't. And it enables us to cultivate our intuition.

In short, self-reflection increases our level of self-awareness. And by learning about ourselves, we can make decisions that are more likely to lead us to the life we desire. By gathering more pieces of the puzzle, we can start to reveal the bigger picture.

In a world full of distractions and "opportunities", the key to a meaningful life is self-reflection.

Wishing we hadn't worked so hard

According to the nurse, Bronnie Ware, one of the five regrets of the dying is that they wish they hadn't worked so hard.

But is that so?

Working is one of the ways we express ourselves and give our gifts to the world. In fact, it could even be argued that we have a moral obligation to do our best work and share it with others.

I suspect that what people truly mean is that they wish they had spent more time doing *meaningful* work.

It all depends on what we mean by "work".

Measuring our life

Some people assess their success based on how much money they make or accumulate. Others judge their life based on the quality of the work they produce. Yet others give more importance to their relationships.

So, how should we measure our life? And how can we make sure we use the proper indicators to evaluate our life satisfaction and move in the right direction?

For instance, how will we measure the following:

- Our mental and physical health,
- Our level of fulfilment,
- The depth and quality of our romantic relationships,
- Our relationships with our family,
- How aligned we are with our mission,
- Our career satisfaction, and
- Our financial success.

There is no right answer that works for everybody, but we'll have to figure out what works for *us*. Otherwise, we won't be able to find the right targets to aim for.

WALKING

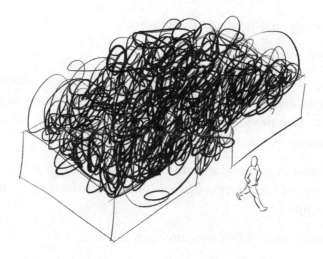

When you feel sad or angry, go for a walk.

When you feel uninspired, go for a walk.

When you feel overwhelmed, go for a walk.

When you're out of shape, go for a walk.

When you can't find a solution to your problems, go for a walk.

Walking enhances your creativity, improves your mood, and provides many health benefits.

When in doubt, walk.

10

ON MASTERY

Loving what we do vs. doing what we love

The more we know about something, the more interesting it tends to become. Sometimes, it's not so much about doing what we love, but about loving what we do. As we become better, we start feeling good about ourselves and want to experience that positive feeling again. As a result, a skill or a job we didn't like at first may become enjoyable.

That's why mastery is so powerful. When we make a conscious choice to master something, we derive more pleasure from doing that thing, we feel more motivated and our life becomes more meaningful as a result.

Human beings are goal-oriented biological creatures. When we direct our natural urge to grow toward mastery, our life tends to improve. As the saying goes, when we improve, everything improves for us.

Mastery is self-discovery

As we strive for excellence, we discover more about ourselves. Watching TV all day won't teach us much about ourselves, but seeking to become the best sushi chef, painter or film producer possible will teach us a great deal.

In short, mastery leads to self-discovery, and self-discovery leads to self-mastery. Mastery of our craft is mastery of ourselves. Therefore, mastery is self-mastery.

(Not so) common sense

If you want to be a writer, write.

If you want to be a coach, coach.

If you want to be a painter, paint.

This is common sense.

Yet, instead of doing the very thing they need to do to reach their goals, many people look for an alternative—a shortcut. They think others know things that they don't. They believe they're missing something. But such behavior is usually an excuse. It's yet another attempt to postpone the fact that they're going to have to do the work.

There is no shortcut. You can't be a professional writer, outstanding coach or talented painter without putting in the hours. You will have to spend thousands of hours honing your craft. The good news is that doing the work will solve most of your problems.

In a distracted world where people are looking for shortcuts or for the next trend, just do the work.

Masters vs. amateurs

Masters take no shortcuts. They do the hard work consistently. They are patient and spend years refining their craft. Because they excel at what they do, instead of being the ones who seek, they end up becoming the ones sought after.

Amateurs seek loopholes. They want to reach success quickly and with the minimum work. Because they're mediocre at what they do, they need to use manipulative tactics to make themselves look more capable. Instead of being sought after, they must continuously seek, whether it is customers, fame or money.

Let's decide whether we want to seek or be sought. Then, let's act accordingly.

10 years

It is said that it takes 10 years to become good at anything. If we seek to master a skill, let's give ourselves 10 years. This will change our approach to everything we do. Similarly, if we want to make money doing what we love, let's give ourselves 10 years. It might take less time, but we'll be prepared.

It could take 10 years to become good. And that's just the beginning.

Infinite progress

Do you plan on working out well into your 60s?

Do you want to be writing, painting or drawing for as long as you can?

Would you like your business to exist and be thriving a few decades from now?

It can be useful to think in terms of infinite progress. To do so entails deciding to improve until the day we die (or for as long as we can).

Infinite progress has no expiration date. Thinking in terms of infinite progress enables us to derive more pleasure from the process than from the (potential) results. It enables us to win every day instead of winning some days (perhaps).

Infinite progress is the antidote to impatience.

When we love the journey more than the destination, we get more joy out of what we do each day. And we make continual and consistent progress.

Forever.

The definition of greatness

Greatness manifests when ordinary people decide to do extraordinary things. Ultimately, it's a choice. It demands that we answer the following question:

"Am I willing to do what it takes to build an extraordinary life and achieve extraordinary things?"

The truth is, for many of us the answer will likely be "no", which is perfectly fine.

Letting our work speak for itself

Outstanding work generates word-of-mouth buzz and sells itself for the most part. Mediocre work requires continuous convincing and endless promotions.

Producing outstanding work people love is difficult though. It requires years of dedication and some luck along the way. But if we feel inclined to do so, it's worth giving it a shot.

Getting eyeballs

Just because we're one of the best in our field doesn't necessarily mean we'll become popular, make a great living or have any kind of impact on society.

For instance, we could be posting better and more useful content than the most successful creatives in our field and fail to gain traction for years.

In truth, we won't be able to generate word-of-mouth buzz unless we can bring enough eyeballs to our work. We might need to put our work in front of 1,000 people. Or it could need to be seen by 10,000, 100,000 or even a million people. That's why "build it and they will come" is only partially true. Great work is essential, but it doesn't guarantee success.

The key is to be honest with ourselves and gather enough feedback to figure out whether the issue is lack of quality or lack of visibility.

The subjectivity of great work

We may love our creation, but others may not. The problem arises when we expect people to love our work, see us as geniuses or throw money at us.

I enjoyed writing this book, but it doesn't mean people will enjoy reading it or that they will find it useful. I can't expect that from readers. The world doesn't owe me anything, and it doesn't owe you or anyone else anything either.

The bottom line is, we can't force others to love our work. Our craft may be world-class in terms of quality, techniques used and aesthetics, and still fail to pique interest.

That's just the way life works.

Doing great work

Doing great work can give us a sense of pride and fulfillment. It can enable us to express our unique talents and gifts, and share them with the world. But nobody will tell us to do our best work. And we will always have something better or more urgent to do at work or in our personal life.

Having said that, we must realize that we might never be able to escape the inner voice that says we must put something out in this world.

Composing a masterpiece, writing beautiful poetry or creating a Greek-like sculpture is somewhat of an impossible task.

In our attempt to create work we're proud of, we'll be discouraged. We'll feel hopeless at times. We'll look at the work of masters and think there is no way we can ever create work of the same caliber. We're simply not good enough. It may lead us to feel jealous or resentful—and we might quit. The task just feels insurmountable.

And it probably is.

But does that mean we shouldn't try? In many regards, the quality of the work we create today and whether it will be appreciated by millions of people or just a few isn't up to us. Our present self cannot know that. Nor can it comprehend the level of growth we may go through in the coming years.

Therefore, let's not compare ourselves with people who have more experience, more knowledge or more time to work on their craft.

Let's simply start where we are and do our best today.

KNOWLEDGE, EXPERIENCE AND WISDOM

LEARN

DO

REFLECT

Knowledge is what we know. Experience is what we do. Wisdom is what we know to be true based on what we've experienced.

If we want to increase our knowledge, we must *learn*.

If we want to gain experience, we must *do*.

If we want to cultivate wisdom, we must *reflect*.

Expressing ourselves through great work

"I am not good enough."

"There are already millions of books, songs or paintings out there."

"Everything has already been said."

We'll probably entertain these thoughts as we attempt to do great work, but we must then let them go. Such thoughts are not useful.

Let's remember that there will never be anyone exactly like us. Accomplishing great work is neither about copying nor about being better than others. It's about sharing our unique insights, creativity, perspectives and passion with our audience.

It's about being *ourselves*.

And no one else but us can do that.

If we feel the desire to do great work, let's start now. Then, let the path work on us more than we work on it. Let's use our journey toward mastery as fuel for our personal growth.

Mastery as a way out

When we commit to mastering one or two skills and become truly extraordinary, many of our issues will go away. We'll begin to make more money, marketing our products, services or ourselves will become easier, and we'll probably feel better about ourselves too.

We might not be good enough yet at our craft, but with a genuine desire for mastery and a lot of patience, we likely will become good enough. And, as we do, everything will tend to become easier.

Fake it until you make it?

If we need to pay thousands of dollars to get featured as a "successful" entrepreneur on a prominent website, purchase fake followers or name drop on every occasion, perhaps we shouldn't be in business.

Instead of faking it until we make it, let's become exceptional at what we do and let word of mouth work for us. Or let's state our goals and then embark on an authentic journey that we share with our audience.

Truth is, we probably aren't skilled enough (yet) in our field of interest. The best thing to do is usually to polish our craft and be patient, but that's not what we want to hear so we'd rather search for the magic pill.

Is it the best we can do?

We may wish to be better, smarter or more confident. But wishful thinking doesn't change our present reality. We are where we are right now. The question we should ask ourselves is: "Is this the best I can do in this very moment"? Over time, our best will improve, and perhaps it will take us to places we would never have expected.

11

ON USING OUR STRENGTHS

Doing what works for us

Just because something works for others doesn't mean the same thing will work for *us*. The best strategy in the world is useless if we can't make it work. We have our unique path to walk. If we ignore our path, we'll be bouncing from one "good" strategy, "sound" idea or "promising" project to the next without moving any closer to where we want to be.

The only solution is self-awareness, self-knowledge and continuous experimentation.

Now, it's difficult to accept that nobody can tell us how we should live our lives and that there may not even be a clear answer. But learning to listen to ourselves and experimenting in the real world is our best shot at moving closer to the future we aspire to.

We must experiment with many things before we can figure out what works for us.

So be it.

Focusing on our strength

Identifying our biggest strength and making the most of it can sometimes yield extraordinary results, transform our life and impact the world at a level we could never have imagined.

Perhaps our soothing voice—when used to narrate videos—can enable us to reach millions of people. Perhaps our ability to synthesize information can enable us to make complex topics accessible and spread knowledge at scale. Or perhaps our empathy can enable us to connect with people at a deeper level and help improve their lives in wonderful ways.

We often have an unfair advantage. But we must find it.

Our unfair advantage

Someone who is good in front of a camera can put a video online and gather thousands of views on their first video. Meanwhile, someone who is camera shy might spend months recording dozens of videos and fail to reach that level.

Someone who is good at learning foreign languages might become fluent in multiple languages while someone else may struggle to learn just one.

Someone who is good at singing might become a famous singer while someone else might sing out of tune and make little progress despite great effort.

Of course, talent alone isn't enough, but when we're naturally good at something and enjoy it, it's far easier to keep going and improve. It's what gives us an unfair advantage over time.

Although it may take months to achieve the results we want, if we focus on our biggest strengths and keep improving, we'll see positive results in the long term. When we're good at something, enjoy it and never give up, the odds tend to be on our side.

Our strengths are invisible (to us)

We notice what's hard, but not so much what's easy. We remember how hard we had to study for a math exam, but not how we aced our English test while barely studying. By design, what comes naturally to us feels natural. That is, we don't see it as anything out of the ordinary. Because it feels so natural to us, we can't imagine how it couldn't be to anyone else. That's an inevitable blind spot we have as humans. We think people are like us, whereas in truth:

- For some, reading might be the most natural thing to do. For others, it might be exhausting.
- For some, speaking in public might be enjoyable. For others, it might be terrifying.
- For some, they feel at home at any party. For others, they feel lonely in a crowd.

When we do what comes easy to us, life tends to become easier, and success feels within our reach. When we do what feels to us like a constant struggle, life tends to be difficult, and every day becomes a new battle.

Playing to our strengths might be the way out.

Feedback is our friend

When we excel at something, the world notices. So, let's pay attention. Is our video gathering a lot of views? Are people willing to pay for our paintings? Was the party we organized a massive success?

Feedback is our antidote against delusion. Let's seek it, learn from it and improve.

Intuition

Intuition is our soul (or mind) telling us that we're moving toward or veering away from what is good for us. The more experience we have —and the more we reflect on them—the better our intuition will become. As we learn to trust our intuition, we stop relying on the opinions of others to live our life. This is when we become true independent thinkers.

When we're young, we must learn from others. But, as we age and grow to know ourselves better, we must liberate ourselves from the opinions of others. The best artists start by copying the work of masters, but they don't stop there. They figure out their unique path so that they can express their creativity. Similarly, we must follow our unique path so that we can express ourselves.

That's what we call "intuition". And that's why other people's advice can only take us so far.

INTUITION IS OUR COMPASS

Intuition is the inner compass that guides us by helping us identify:

What we should be doing,

What we believe is right for us, and

What we think will work for us.

Doing what we love

We might not like our current job, but we can always find time each day to do a little bit more of what we love.

If we don't start there, what else is there to do?

Weaknesses as strengths

What if we start seeing our biggest weaknesses as our ultimate strengths?

My introversion and shyness led me to observe and listen more, which enabled me to gather more insight and deepen my wisdom, which enabled me to create insightful books people can benefit from.

I can perceive my French accent as a liability and spend hours trying to "fix" it. Or I can see it as an asset that enables me to stand out among the native English speakers in my field.

I can see my somewhat obsessive personality as a bad thing and let it consume me by obsessing over the wrong things. Or I can direct it toward something I love and find meaningful, use it to amplify my talents and skills, and contribute to society in a productive way.

The point is, we can lament our so-called weaknesses, or we can ask ourselves how we can make them work for us.

Looking at the big picture may enable us to see our weaknesses in a new and more constructive light. Or they may have a humbling effect and teach us to collaborate with others who possess the strengths we lack.

Our weaknesses are what makes us unique. Nobody wants to be around someone who is perfect. If Superman didn't have his kryptonite, there wouldn't be any story worth telling. Similarly, if we didn't have our Achilles' heel, our life wouldn't be as interesting and meaningful. Having weaknesses is being human. Weaknesses enable us to relate to others and create deeper, more meaningful connections. And what is life without deep, intimate relationships?

Having weaknesses makes us vulnerable, and vulnerability makes us human.

Let's be more human.

Trying hard (or not)

If we need to try so hard, perhaps we're on the wrong path.

- If we need to try so hard to sell our product, perhaps we're selling the wrong product, or we're selling it to the wrong people.
- If we need to try so hard at work, perhaps we're in the wrong job, company or industry.
- If we need to try so hard to convince someone to be with us, perhaps they're the wrong person for us.

Perseverance has its place, but not everything has to be hard.

If every day feels like a continuous struggle, let's look for the path of least resistance. Let's see if we can go where our talent, skills and personality are appreciated, where we can enjoy what we're doing, and where people appreciate and value us.

If it's that hard, perhaps we're in the wrong place.

What we do for fun

When seeking to build a business, let's observe what we do for fun in our spare time. Perhaps, we could turn it into a business. If it doesn't work, we'll have learned new skills, and we will have grown. If it's successful, we'll be doing something we love for a living. Plus, by doing what we love, we won't give up easily during tough times.

DOING MORE OF WHAT WE LOVE

You might not love everything you do, but you should try doing most of the things you love.

12

ON CREATIVITY

Creativity and self-expression

Creativity is the art of putting part of ourselves in what we do. Because we're all unique, we can all find ways to express our creativity.

Everybody can be creative

Marketing can be creative. Sales can be creative. Customer service can be creative. Many problems have creative solutions too.

Being creative is being human. It's using our thinking that has resulted from past experiences, interactions, learned skills and unique perspectives to do something differently.

We can all be creative.

Everything has been said before

Because "everything has been said before" doesn't mean we shouldn't try to say something new or introduce an existing concept in a unique way.

The most valuable concepts and ideas take time to be digested. People need to be exposed to the same concept many times before they understand it. Our unique way to explain a concept, or our unique life experiences may touch someone else like nothing has before. Or it may reveal to them the deeper meaning of a key concept they have heard multiple times before. It's what we refer to as having an "aha moment".

That's why the recycling and repackaging of old concepts isn't superfluous. It's necessary. In marketing, it is said that, on average, it takes seven interactions with a product or brand before people buy. In a similar way, it takes multiple encounters with a concept before people can make it their own.

Repeating similar concepts using different words, stories and examples increases the odds that people will internalize key ideas that can transform their lives. It destroys the "I already know that" syndrome many of us fall prey to—i.e., the idea we know something deeply while we merely know it intellectually.

For instance, it might take time for us to realize that we can learn almost any skill we need to reach any goal we have. Even if we believe it, we may not have yet internalized that truth. Or it could take us years to grasp the importance of consistency. We may stick to a routine for a few weeks, or perhaps even a few months while failing to realize the astonishing power of remaining consistent for years. Once we do, our entire outlook on life can change drastically.

The bottom line is, if something piques our interest, let's share it with others. If we have something to say, let's say it with our own words. Others may find it useful.

Bringing something new to the world

At first, we have no choice but to mimic others. We need points of reference on which to base our work. During the formative stage, we're unsure of our own voice. We often think we are better than we really are, but over time, we find our voice and allow ourselves to rely less and less on what others are doing.

That's when we begin to be creative.

Let's set the intention to be creative. Yes, a lot of things have already been said or done, but we shouldn't doubt our ability to be creative and bring something original into this world. We might not succeed, but it shouldn't stop us from trying.

Studying vs. creating

If we study too much, we risk being overly influenced by what others have done before us. But if we study too little, we risk not having sufficient knowledge or solid enough foundations to do creative work.

Sometimes, we must dedicate ourselves to the creative process while staying away from external influences. We must give ourselves the room (and the permission) to be creative and to think, feel and experience for ourselves. Other times, we must learn from others, dissect what they are doing and integrate it in our own way.

It's a balancing act.

The benefit of curiosity

A lot of the innovation we see in any field comes from people who bring different perspectives. They often come from a different background and have extensive experiences in an unrelated area.

Let's remain curious. Let's learn from unexpected places. Let's go beyond what we perceive as our field. We can never know what wonderful insights we might gather along the way.

Stop quoting people

As a writer, there is great safety in quoting successful writers. As a painter, it's easier to copy what successful painters have done before. As a content creator, it's convenient to plagiarize popular content. In short, it's more comfortable to hide behind someone else's work rather than stand up for our own work.

As we begin our creative journey, we'll inevitably go down that path. Copying others helps us define the limits of the playing field. It prevents us from getting lost. But it also hinders our creative abilities. Thus, there will come a point where we will have to go our own way.

Plato didn't quote Plato. Picasso didn't imitate Picasso. Beethoven didn't mimic Beethoven. They went their own way.

Being truly authentic and creative means that we're not copying anyone else. If anything, the first sign that we're creative is when others copy *us*.

Mimic —> Integrate —> Transcend

Mimicking is necessary, but it's only the first step. We must integrate and, eventually, transcend.

Mimic —> Integrate —> Transcend.

Let's repeat that cycle over and over.

That's how we'll find our unique voice.

Planning vs. emerging

Creativity isn't a linear process. Creativity is a dynamic process that evolves as we begin the work. We cannot master creativity. We can merely create the conditions for it to emerge.

If we can write an outline for a book and follow it to the letter, we're probably not that creative. If we have an idea for a poem, it's unlikely that it will turn out exactly as we had expected. There will be delightful surprises but also many challenges along the way. And if we have a specific problem to solve, the way we solve it might be wildly different from the one we had in mind.

We can set intentions and plan as best we can, but we probably shouldn't do so to the extent we stifle our creativity. Some amount of open-mindedness and willingness to let go is essential.

The point is, as we enter the creative process, we'll come up with new ideas, which will reshape the original project we had in mind. In other words, we can't plan creativity. We can only give it the space it needs to manifest itself. Then, we must be bold enough and curious enough to let our creativity express itself rather than letting it suffocate.

13

ON SUCCESS

Success is feeling as though we are where we are supposed to be, doing what we're supposed to do. If so, the ultimate sign of success is wanting to be nowhere else but where we are right now.

The recipe to success

The secret to success is that there is no secret. But if I were to give a few pointers, they would be to grow the following:

- Self-awareness so that we know what we're good at and what we value,
- Continuous improvement so that we keep becoming better,
- Humility so that we keep learning,
- Resilience so that we're able to persevere, and
- Passion and drive so that we stay motivated over the long term.

There is no one path

There is seldom one clear path to success. Many things we may believe are a must, often aren't. Below are a few examples:

- We must surround ourselves with the right people. —> It's possible to succeed without being around successful people.
- We must wake at 5 am and have an elaborate morning routine. —> We can succeed without waking up early or having any morning routine.
- We must work 60 or 80 hours a week. —> We can work a few hours a day and be more successful than most people.

The path toward success is not straightforward. Surrounding ourselves with the right people, waking up early, or working hard will be helpful for most of us, but these actions don't guarantee success, nor are they necessarily required to help us reach our goals.

The most important thing is to figure out what works for us.

DISCIPLINING OURSELVES

If we don't discipline ourselves, someone else will.

And we may not like the way they do it.

Focusing

We are what we focus on.

We see what we focus on.

If we aren't making progress toward the life we desire, that's usually because our focus is *not* where it needs to be. As we observe where our focus goes during our day, we will know it to be mostly true.

Savoring our small victories

A big part of our fulfilment comes from how we perceive things, not from what we do. We don't feel ten times more successful by achieving ten times more. In other words, the feeling of success doesn't grow exponentially but obeys the law of diminishing returns. The more success we have, the harder it is to feel it and appreciate it. That's why, many "successful" people continuously chase the next dopamine hit.

In truth, extraordinary success doesn't necessarily lead to deep fulfilment. External success doesn't always translate into internal success. It's only by taking the time to savor our victories (small or big) that we may experience more fulfilment.

Getting what we want (or not)

It is not necessary to think about what we want to obtain.

We can be happy without thinking about happiness. We can make money without obsessing over money. We can be productive without becoming a productivity nerd. In fact, sometimes, thinking about something gets in the way of us obtaining it.

What matters is what we do, *not* just what we think about. Many of the things we want are consequences of our actions. For instance:

- We may find happiness by focusing on doing things we enjoy, engaging in meaningful activities and seeking to challenge ourselves. These things don't require us to think about happiness.

- We may make a lot of money by seeking to provide value to others by using our skills, talents and unique abilities. This doesn't require us to obsess over money.
- Or we may become highly productive by tackling the task in front of us and completing it to the best of our ability, over and over. This doesn't entail us becoming productivity junkies.

We don't necessarily get what we think about. But, perhaps we get what we create processes for.

Life as a math problem

In life, the more shots we take, the more likely we are to succeed. So, by taking just one more "shot" every day for a decade, we mathematically increase our chances of achieving success in whatever goal we may pursue.

Therefore, life is largely a game of probability. The more we do, the luckier we tend to become.

Life as a simulation game

In the simulation we call "life", for a large part, our confidence determines whether our character will reach level 100 or stay stuck at level 1. As we level up, many of the things we desire may become possible.

How much control we have over our mind determines the level we reach. The more we master our mind, the bigger our field of possibility becomes. This might be one of the few universal truths.

Let's strive to master our mind and create more options in our lives.

DOING THE WORK

Most of what we do isn't going to work.

But it's important that *we* do the work.

Success and pride

Pride is the enemy of success. When we want to look good, be right or protect a certain sense of self, we limit our growth.

Many people fail in business and life because of a misguided sense of pride. They'd rather be right than accept that what they're doing doesn't work and make the necessary changes. One of the keys to living a better life is to learn from our mistakes more often and faster so that we can realign our actions with our goals. We need to value learning over being right.

People who can self-correct effectively and accept being wrong, or even look stupid from time to time, tend to do better in life. On the other hand, people with too much pride remain stuck. They cling to an old identity that isn't serving them well.

In a complex world, our ability to self-reflect and learn from our mistakes enables us to adapt and reach our goals.

The top 1%

To be in the top 1%, whether in the amount of money we earn, the quality of our relationships or our mental or physical health, we must do what most people can't or won't do.

This doesn't necessarily mean that it will be hard or impossible, but it does entail thinking differently and holding ourselves to a higher standard than the average person. It starts by finding what being in the top 1% requires, and then, making it the norm for us (i.e., raising our standards).

After all, who decides what our standard should be?

We do.

We are the ones deciding what we want our life to be and what standards we need to set to attain our goals.

Getting the foundations right

Great companies build outstanding products and attract the best talent, which gives them strong foundations on which to grow their business. Similarly, successful people build their lives on rock-solid foundations—genuine long-term relationships, a high level of education, valuable skills, curiosity, patience and a thirst for self-improvement.

Conversely, unsuccessful people try to take advantage of others, jump on trends or look for "shortcuts". In short, their life is built on quicksand. That's why, from their perspective, the target always seems to be moving. Because they have shaky foundations, everything they do becomes unstable. Long-term plans are replaced with short-term activities, strategy with busyness, and focus with endless distractions. Unsurprisingly, they never seem to go far.

While successful people may occasionally surf on trends to increase their success, for unsuccessful people, trends are all they have. They think success is all about seizing the right opportunity. But, in truth, it's more about having the right foundations in place. With solid foundations, everything we do works better, which helps us move closer to our long-term goals. With weak foundations, nothing we do seems to work.

Let's make sure we establish strong foundations on which we can build the life we desire.

The retirement dream

We often wait for retirement to do the things we've always wanted to do, whether it is traveling the world, pursuing new hobbies or spending more time with our family.

That's a bad strategy.

For one thing, we don't know what our health will be like. We may not have as much energy as we currently have. Or we may suffer from arthritis, chronic diseases or poor sleep. There is also a real risk that we won't live long enough to enjoy retirement at all. We simply don't know what the future will bring. With that in mind, let's reevaluate our current priorities.

Now, it doesn't mean we shouldn't plan and prepare for retirement. But it does mean we should be more intentional with what we do each day and seek ways to do the things we enjoy most sooner rather than later.

Playing to win

Life is a game that we can play in many ways. It is important that we play to win, which means:

- **Focusing on what we're good at and what we enjoy.** When we play to our strengths and do more of what we love, it feels as though we are in the right place and doing what we're supposed to do.
- **Going where we're valued and where people need us.** Value is subjective. Some people will love us, others will hate us. Some people will value our work and what we have to say, but others won't care less. Let's go where we feel valued.
- **Listening to what the world tells us.** The world will give us feedback. It will tell us what we're good at, what our unique abilities are and where people need us most. Let's listen very carefully.
- **Falling in love with the process.** We can't always achieve the outcome we want, but we can decide to keep growing and learning. We can win by focusing on the process and doing the best we can each day.

Life is a game. But it sometimes takes a lifetime to figure out the rules and to play to win on our own terms.

The best predictor of success

We live in a short-term world ruled by ten-second videos, clickbait content, 24/7 news and get-rich-quick schemes. All of these push us to think short term and be impatient, which, ultimately, leads to mediocrity. Nothing great can ever be built without an extraordinary amount of time and effort. The completion of meaningful projects always requires sustained focus and long-term thinking.

That's why the best predictor of success is long-term thinking. When we expand our time horizon, we turn the odds in our favor. Thinking long-term impacts every action we take starting today and, thus, inevitably changes our future. Long-term thinking is how we achieve extraordinary results.

As a rule of thumb, how far into the future we think is directly proportionate to our level of success. We can't have extraordinary success if we think in terms of days or weeks. We must think in terms of years, or even better, decades.

Life is a marathon, not a sprint

Patience is often a virtue we appreciate as we grow older. Yet its benefits would be most felt when we are young.

For instance, investing in our twenties is far more impactful than investing in our forties. Our money has a couple more decades to compound and turn into a life-changing sum. Similarly, young people who invest their energy in learning useful skills will likely build a more fulfilling career over the long term.

Life is a marathon. The earlier we start running, the further we will go. But, regardless of our age, by thinking long term and taking small steps each day, we'll move closer to our goals.

We don't have to sprint. But we do have to keep putting one foot in front of the other.

One step at a time

Let's start leaning more toward what we love doing and what interests us. We don't need to know (yet) how we will get there. We often can't.

Taking the first step is the best strategy for designing the life we desire. Let's act now before we run out of time.

The power of *not*

Not losing money can make us rich.

Not giving up on our business for a decade can make us successful.

Not eating bad food can enable us to stay fit and healthy.

Not injuring ourselves can help us get in great shape after a few years of working out.

All these things compound over the years. They are like an investment. And it becomes easier and easier to maintain our gain over time. It is:

- Easier to maintain wealth than to build it,
- Easier to maintain a thriving business than to create one,
- Easier to maintain our ideal weight than to lose weight, and it is
- Easier to maintain our level of fitness than to get in shape.

Showing up. Being consistent. Focusing on *not* losing. That's one of the best ways to design the life we want.

That's the power of *not*.

Intensity vs. consistency

Sometimes, we're willing to give it 100% to make progress fast. But, by trying so hard, we often end up burning out in one way or another.

- By training too hard, we risk injuring ourselves and wiping out months of training.
- By working too hard on our business, we may burn out, forcing us to take a break for weeks or even months.
- By being too strict with our diet, we often end up throwing in the towel.

It's better to give it 80-to-90% consistently than to give it 100% inconsistently. Small steady progress is usually far more effective than fast progress followed by injuries, burnout or involuntary breaks.

In the end, the small and sometimes almost invisible progress we make on a daily or weekly basis leads to exponential results over the long term.

Everything is about habits

Most of the results we obtain in life are the results of what we do consistently—i.e., habits. And habits have a far wider reach than we think. In truth, almost everything is a habit (or can be turned into one).

- Good thinking is a habit (as is poor thinking).
- Gratitude is a habit (as is a sense of entitlement).
- Decisiveness is a habit (as is indecisiveness).
- Focus is a habit (as is a lack of focus).
- Discipline is a habit (as is laziness).

Through consistency we can transform not only what we do, but also how we think and feel. Ultimately, the difference between a fulfilling life and an unfulfilling one lies in the quality of our habits.

Everything is about habits. When our daily habits move us closer to the ideal life we want, we will often succeed.

Push and pull

We can't be pushing all the time. "Hustling" has its place, but we must also learn to stop, let go and allow things to unfold. We must alternate between push and pull. We do so by switching between getting things done (desire for control) and relaxing, having faith and not forcing anything (willingness to let go). When we push, we show the world how serious we are by doing the hard work. When we pull, we let go of our desire for control and accept that there are forces at play bigger than ourselves.

Yet, many of us continually push, trying to hustle our way to success. We heard that we should work 14 hours a day, 7 days a week—so that's what we do. Working hard gives us a sense of control. We're doing something. We're moving forward. And by being busy, we don't have to think too much. We don't have time to worry whether we'll reach our target.

But the truth is, people aren't machines. We can't work all the time. We need time away from work to process the enormous amount of information we're exposed to. We also need time to recover so that we can use the full range of our mental capacities when we work.

If we've been pushing for too long, perhaps it's time to pull.

Busyness vs. resting

Busyness leads to the implementation of too many tactics, often ineffective ones.

Resting enables us to make useful connections in our brain. It helps us differentiate signal (useful content) from noise (unnecessary information).

By giving ourselves room to zoom out, we can craft better strategies that can be far more effective than any short-term tactics we could ever implement.

Building a library of mental models

Wading through information that we won't be "using" isn't necessarily a waste of time. Every book we read or video we watch can expose us to someone else's perspective on the world. Consuming information is how we get to live the lives of thousands of people, whether fictional or real.

If we only have a few mental models in our library, we will look at things in a simplistic way. We will lack the perspective needed to approach issues the right way. As the saying goes, when we have only a hammer, everything looks like a nail. But as we absorb more information and reflect, we increase our library of mental models— our problem-solving toolkit—and, as a result, we have more tools available when it comes to making decisions. By accumulating hundreds of mental models over time, we become far better equipped to tackle complex issues, we can make wiser decisions and ultimately make our goals easier to reach.

To expand our library of mental models, we can read biographies, analyze how we solved past problems or observe how people around us deal with their challenges.

WE CAN BE SUCCESSFUL TODAY

Success is a process.

So long as we're striving to move toward our life goals, we're successful.

And we can start *today*.

The best assumption

Perhaps the fastest way to get rid of "limiting beliefs" is to let go of that concept altogether. In other words, it's best to assume that we *can* do anything we want and then, through our actions, prove it can (or cannot) be done. Otherwise, how are we to know what is or isn't possible for us?

In short, we can try to eliminate a never-ending flow of limiting beliefs one by one. Or we can start with the general assumption that we can do anything we want, live our lives accordingly and see what unfolds.

A few rules of thumb

Follow these rules. They will save you a lot of time and effort.

- Wait at least 24 hours before buying anything expensive.
- Seek experts, don't let them seek you. A true expert in their domain is the one sought after, not the one doing the seeking.
- Don't invest in what you don't understand (or make sure it's a fraction of your investment portfolio).
- If it doesn't feel right, don't do it. Don't follow people's advice if it doesn't resonate with you.
- If you wouldn't want it done to you, don't do it to someone else.
- If it seems too good to be true, it probably is.
- If it doesn't require much of your time and effort, it's probably not worth it. Anything of value takes time and effort.

The confidence paradox

On one hand, we want to be confident so that we can move toward our biggest goals and create the life we want. On the other hand, the more we learn, the more we realize how little we know about anything.

That's the confidence paradox.

Solving the confidence paradox

The key to solving the confidence paradox might be to believe in our ability to learn and grow, while staying humble. It might be to realize that we know little and that there is always more to learn. This entails being willing to let go of pride and ego and admit whenever we're wrong. By doing so, we can keep moving toward our goals while continually learning.

In other words, we should believe that we can learn anything required to reach our goals—that we can figure things out. However, at the same time, we should also accept that the process to get us to our goals will be chaotic and profoundly humbling.

14

ON GOALS AND MOTIVATION

Goals are merely tools for growth.

Let's select goals that turn us into better people. By doing so we can never truly fail.

In other words, let's trade our expectations of success for expectations of personal growth and meaningful learning.

We won't always reach our goals, but we will certainly grow.

Journey vs. destination

Who we become as we move towards our goals is far more important than whether we reach all our goals at all. Goals are games we choose to play. They are personal development tools. Therefore, some of the key questions to ask are:

- Are we polishing our craft?
- Are we moving beyond our comfort zone?
- Are we learning more about ourselves?
- Are we getting closer to the life we desire?
- Are we becoming more patient, wise and compassionate?

The achievement of our dreams, even the wildest ones, seldom provides us with the sense of fulfilment we're looking for. We are then left with the person we became in the process of attaining those dreams. Therefore, before anything else, we should make sure that reaching our goals will help us become a better person—a person we can be proud of.

Ultimately, success is a process. We're successful when we pursue worthy endeavors that enable us to feel good about ourselves. Whether we achieve our goals isn't always within our control.

Short-term failure, long-term success

While we may fail to reach our goals in the short term, we may achieve extraordinary results in the long term. As the saying goes, we often overestimate what we can do in one year, but underestimate what we can do in a decade.

Therefore, let's trade our short-term expectations for long-term ones. We can accomplish wonderful things in the coming years.

But let's also expect many "failures" along the way.

The simplest goal-setting method

Write down the following things on separate pieces of paper:

- Your 5- or 10-year vision.

- What you must achieve this year to move toward it.
- What you will do in the next 90 days to reach your yearly goals.
- What you will do this month to reach your 90-day goals.
- What you will do this week to reach your monthly goals.
- What you will do today to reach your weekly goals.

Each morning, spend a couple of minutes to review your 90-day, monthly and weekly goals. This will make sure you're on the right track. Then, set your goals for the day.

No app. No complex system. Just a pen and a few sheets of paper.

This method will work wonders for most people. And whoever sticks to it consistently for long enough, will dramatically increase their productivity.

Seeking clarity

Achieving clarity is a never-ending process. It's normal to be unsure of what we like, what our passion is or what we should be doing. We gain clarity over time by *acting* and *reflecting*.

Acting is necessary because it enables us to receive feedback from the world. Are we going in the right direction? Do we enjoy what we're doing? Are we good at it? And so on.

In many cases, lack of clarity can be cured through action, which entails:

- Taking the first step toward a worthy goal,
- Tackling the immediate problem(s) in front of us,
- Leaning in toward what we're curious about, and
- Doing more of what we love each day.

Reflecting is essential because it enables us to extract deeper lessons from our actions and from the ensuing feedback. It helps us become more self-aware, which is an essential component to living a good life.

Act.

Reflect.

Rinse and repeat.

That's how you will gain clarity.

It starts with "why"

The main reason we fail to reach our goals is that we don't really want them. To achieve our biggest goals, we must figure out what exactly they are and why they matter to us. When we have a strong enough "why", the "how" tends to take care of itself.

Too much motivation

Feeling motivated gives us the impression that we're doing something. As a result, it reduces our propensity to act.

That's the trap of motivation.

We can read uplifting books or watch motivational videos to keep us going when it's hard, but most of the time, we should "simply" focus on doing the work needed to obtain the results we want.

Doing is usually better than seeking inspiration.

A few words on perseverance

Grit begins when we decide to keep going while most people in the same situation would have given up. Any time before that we're just behaving like everybody else.

Let's not expect extraordinary results when acting like most people.

Thoughts on ambition

There seems to be a direct correlation between the amount of trauma and insecurities in our lives and our level of ambition. Extremely "successful" people seem to have an insatiable desire to prove others wrong or to show the world that they are good enough and worthy of love. It's the fuel that keeps them going.

The question is then, can we be wildly successful without having deep childhood traumas or severe insecurities? In other words, if we have little to prove to the world, why would we try to build a billion-dollar company, become a prominent politician or break a world record?

I do not know.

Perhaps the answer lies in the pursuit of mastery, in seeking joy in honing our craft and in a deep love of learning. When combined with a strong desire to be useful to others, it can fuel our ambition and enable us to reach greatness.

Why should we?

One of my friends is torn between his ambition for more and his desire to enjoy what he is blessed with. He raises a good point. Why should we try to achieve more? Why should we work harder? Why should we constantly seek to become better?

This is a question I've been wrestling with for a while. But there is another way to think about it:

Why *shouldn't* we?

- Why have average health when we could have vibrant health?
- Why be physically weak when we could be strong?
- Why do mediocre work when we could become extraordinary at what we do and feel proud of ourselves?
- Why have little impact on the world when we could impact the lives of thousands or millions of people?
- Why be poor when we could be wealthy?

We have a choice. We can decide who we want to be. The key lies in honesty. We must not lie to ourselves regarding our personal ambitions. However, we must do the work necessary to make them come true.

Perhaps a good question to clarify where we stand is:

Do I want more but pretend otherwise because I'm afraid of failure or unwilling to do the work? Or am I genuinely happy with what I currently have?

Appreciating what we have is key, but it doesn't mean we should stop growing and pursuing worthy goals.

Past, present and future

The concepts we call "past", "present" and "future" exist because of our ability to imagine, remember and store memories. In truth, only the present moment is real. But "you should live in the now" is a piece of advice few of us know what to do with.

Now, we might not be able to run away from these concepts of "past", "present" and "future", but we can certainly learn to use them in a more constructive way.

We can use our past to:

- Relive fond memories,
- Celebrate our accomplishments, and
- Learn invaluable lessons.

We can use our future to:

- Visualize the life we want, and
- Get excited about our goals.

And we can use the present to:

- Motivate us to act now by learning from the past, remembering our accomplishments and visualizing our goals, and
- Create a detailed action plan to reach those goals.

This is the opposite of what many of us tend to do, which is to:

- Dwell on past mistakes and failures, and

- Worry about the future.

Weaknesses vs. strengths

As a leader, when we promote our strengths, we stimulate other people's egos and their desire to strive for more. On the other hand, when we broadcast our weaknesses, we touch other people's hearts and encourage them to embrace their humanity. In the first case, we often leave people feeling inadequate. In the second case, we help them accept their flaws and inadequacies, and carry their burdens. Paradoxically, in doing so, we make it easier for them to overcome their personal issues and reach their potential.

Being vulnerable isn't necessary a weakness. Sometimes, it can be a strength.

Confidence vs. delusion

Too much confidence becomes overconfidence, which can turn into delusion. Delusional people have a distorted vision of their own abilities. As a result, they can spend years making little progress toward their vision while genuinely believing the breakthrough they've been waiting for is just around the corner.

How can we avoid becoming such people?

Perhaps the key lies in cultivating a deep sense of humility coupled with the realization that we know little about the world. We should also pay close attention to the feedback we receive regarding our work and our current abilities.

15

ON PRODUCTIVITY

Perhaps the ultimate point of productivity is to free our time so that we can do "unproductive" things we love with people we care about.

The essence of productivity

Put simply, productivity is our ability to make our time more valuable —i.e., to achieve bigger results in less time and effort. Now, it doesn't necessarily entail working longer hours or completing more tasks. In truth, we can't:

- Flip burgers ten times faster,
- Increase tenfold the number of hours we work per week, or
- Make ten times more sales calls per day.

Being productive means that we must do things differently.

The true currency of the world

We can have all the time in the world, but if we are bedridden, in tremendous pain or lethargic, what's the point? The true currency of the world is not time, it's energy.

Therefore, managing our energy is the most important thing we can do.

Managing our energy

A large majority of us don't need complex productivity systems. Instead, we need to master the basics. Before looking for any productivity trick or tip, we must go back to the fundamentals, which entails:

- Eating better food,
- Sleeping longer and more effectively, and
- Working out regularly.

Most of us could be doing better in one or several of these areas. Improving on any of these points will give us more energy and will boost our productivity.

Productivity and strategy

Without a solid strategy, our productivity will be severely limited. A strategy is a plan we create to gather the resources we need and make sure we allocate them effectively to reach our goals. In the absence of strategy, we often tread water and achieve little.

Exceptional productivity requires an outstanding strategy executed flawlessly.

Effectiveness vs. efficiency

Doing *things right* happens when we stop thinking.

Doing the *right things* happens when we stop and think.

In other words, when we throw ourselves into work without thinking, we end up doing many ineffective or unnecessary tasks efficiently (i.e., we merely do things right). Conversely, when we stop and think of what must be done to reach our goals, we end up working on the right things, which makes us more productive.

Ultimately, doing the *right things* is far more important than doing *things right*.

Slow is fast

When we focus on the present moment and seek to complete the task in front of us slowly and deliberately, time slows down. Yet, we accomplish more, and we complete tasks faster. This paradox shows that doing more or trying to complete every task as fast as possible is not always the most effective use of our time.

12-hour workdays

Most people don't need to work more than eight hours a day for more than a short time.

People who convince themselves they should work longer hours are often workaholics, or just don't know any better.

When we work long hours, we reach a point where we don't have enough mental bandwidth to think clearly. It often leads us to do unnecessary work, or work that someone else could have done better and faster. In addition, because we're exhausted, a task we could have completed in an hour may now take us three or four. Finally, a long working day leaves little time to think and to rest. And thought and rest are key elements to remaining productive over the long term.

Although working long hours may be necessary *at times*, we need to challenge the idea that it should be the norm or that it is the most effective way to attain our goals.

Working hard vs. working smart

We should work smart, not hard, right?

One problem though:

It's difficult, if not impossible, to work smart if we've never worked hard before.

By working hard, we begin to appreciate the difference between busy work and effective work. This is how we begin to eliminate what's ineffective and focus on what works. All the productive people I know had to work hard (usually for a few years) before they could even hope to work smart. Therefore, if you struggle to work smart, don't worry. You might still be in the learning phase.

If this seems to contradict my previous point, that's because it does (kind of). We often need to spend a few years working long hours to jumpstart our careers or build a business. The key is to learn how to transition from working hard to working smart.

Easier said than done.

The different types of productivity

There isn't one way to be productive. Being productive will vary based on whether we're a blue-collar worker, a white-collar employee, a manager, an artist or an entrepreneur.

For workers on an assembly line, how fast and flawlessly they can repeat the same movement might determine their level of productivity.

For white-collar employees, how well they can complete the assignment they were given might be the critical component of their productivity.

For managers, getting their team to complete projects under budget and on time might be how they are evaluated.

For artists, it could be how many paintings they can create, how good the reviews are or how much money they can sell their art for.

For entrepreneurs, it might be how much profit they make or how many products they sell. Or it could be how fast they're growing their customer base.

In short, to be productive, we must use the right type of productivity at the right place and the right time. And if we desire to be somewhere else, doing something else, we must start thinking about productivity in a different way—a way more aligned with the type of work we want to do or career we aspire to have.

The different productivity modes

We rely on different modes when trying to be productive. Each mode has its place and should be used wisely.

- *The hustle mode* can enable us to get a lot done but it is limiting, forceful and unsustainable. It should be used only when necessary.
- *The strategic mode* helps us ensure we work on the right things. It is deliberate and focused.
- *The creative mode* enables us to do creative work. The words that characterize it best are "expanding" and "effortless".
- *The spiritual mode* enables us to go beyond the physical world and move into the world of imagination. It feels boundless and all-encompassing, offering limitless opportunities.

To be productive, the key might be to alternate between these modes when we feel stuck or feel as though we're constantly hustling. Alternatively, let's zoom out and move toward a more strategic, creative or spiritual mode.

Producers vs. consumers

The internet gives us access to billions of people.

When we use the internet to *capture people's attention*, we can spread our message and impact the world, sometimes at unprecedented levels.

But when we go on the internet to *give away our attention*, we're at the mercy of other people or corporations. They want to convince us of something, whether it is to buy their products or change our behavior.

In the former case, we can be said to be "producers". We put content "out there" to spread a message and, hopefully, provide value to others. In the latter case, we can be said to be "consumers". We use the internet to distract ourselves from a life we aren't satisfied with, or perhaps to look for inspiration and avoid boredom. In doing so, we're largely acting unconsciously, looking for someone or something to grab our attention.

In short, we can be a master of the internet and use it to learn invaluable skills, spread our message, grow our business and generate money. Or we can be its slaves, mindlessly consuming information and letting marketers, and sometimes scammers or narcissists, make us feel insecure so that they can manipulate us.

The internet is just a tool. We must choose how to use it.

Is time working for or against us?

When we use our time wisely, we build, whether it is meaningful relationships, invaluable skills, thriving businesses, wonderful memories or a stronger mind. When we misuse our time, we become lost, wandering through life while failing to create anything meaningful.

Put differently, time works for us when we invest it. By doing so, we activate the miracle of compounding. Our small daily efforts grow into something bigger than we could have ever imagined, be it a more fulfilling career, deeper relationships, greater wealth and so on.

Conversely, time works against us when we waste it, that is when we fail to use it in a meaningful way, when we fail to build anything that lasts.

Time will pass anyway. Let's invest our time and make it work for us, not against us.

The role of deadlines

Deadlines enable us to complete the job when nothing else will. They bring our attention to the fact that our time is limited. When we know something needs to be done by a certain date, we prime our mind to move forward and find ways to complete tasks sooner rather than later.

Without deadlines, most books wouldn't be written, most homework wouldn't be done and most projects wouldn't be completed.

Deadlines activate human creativity, ingenuity, and resourcefulness. They are what enables our soul to leave its imprint on the world before it's too late. When used well, deadlines are a good thing.

Productivity and impact

The more impact our decisions and actions have, the more productive we become. The more irreplaceable we are, the more money we may make (depending on how marketable our skills are). If so, perhaps one way to assess our current level of productivity is to consider:

- How impactful the decisions we make actually are, and
- How easily we can be replaced.

If the decisions we make each day have little impact, perhaps we should ask ourselves what we're going to do about it.

Think and grow more productive

Our level of productivity is directly correlated to our ability to think and the extent to which we use that ability. As a rule of thumb, the more we think, the more likely we are to become more productive, maybe not today or tomorrow, but over time.

The art of saying no

It's okay to say no. It's okay not to reply to every email. It's okay not to be on social media.

We have the right to protect our time so that we can focus on what matters and avoid burnout. People can't expect us always to be available to them. Neither can we expect that from others.

What if we start with the premise that our default answer is no? What if we only say yes to what we are excited about or can support? How much trouble would we save ourselves? How much easier would our life become?

Let's free ourselves and others from the tyranny of endless interactions, constant interruptions and incessant requests.

Let's make "no" our default answer.

More isn't always better

When I studied at business school, I spent most of my waking hours attending classes, reading case studies or working on group projects. I was too tired to think and had no time to digest the information I was exposed to. I've noticed the same patterns at various seminars I've attended.

But when it comes to information, more isn't always better. The desire to pack events, courses or books with tons of information results from fears or misconceptions:

- *The fear of not delivering enough value.* If we don't share with people everything we know, they might feel cheated. Or, if we're not delivering enough value, it means we aren't good enough.
- *The misconception about learning.* The belief that more information is better results from the erroneous comparison with the industrial age where more time on the assembly

line meant more work done. But the same logic doesn't necessarily apply today.

These days, what matters most isn't the *amount* of content we consume, but its quality, its relevance to our situation and how well we're able to use it to reach our goals.

More isn't always better.

The power of the 80/20 Principle

The 80/20 Principle is the most powerful framework. We should study it extensively and use it as often as possible in various areas of our lives. This principle states that 20% of our actions result in 80% of our outcome. Or, more generally, some actions have a disproportionate impact.

Below are a few examples:

- 20% of our actions toward a specific goal brings 80% of our results.
- 20% of our customers generates 80% of our profits.
- 20% of the world's population owns 80% of the wealth.
- 20% of our problems creates 80% of the stress we experience.

Of course the ratio isn't always 80/20. This is just a guideline. The ratio may be 70/15, 90/10 or even 99/1.

So, why is it the most powerful framework?

Because focus is our biggest asset.

The 80/20 Principle helps us channel our focus by reminding us that, in life, not everything matters equally. There are always some things that matter more than others.

Now, while the 80/20 Principle is incredibly effective, it seldom comes naturally. It might be because of the way we learn. At school, we're taught to complete our homework indiscriminately. At no point are we asked to sort out tasks by order of importance. We carry that same mindset well into adulthood. At work, we complete our tasks without considering their relevance or effectiveness—or we simply do what we're told to do because we must. If we ever decide to create our own business, we adopt a similar mindset. But unfortunately, the traditional to-do list doesn't lead to extraordinary results.

It's only through consistent practice and a lot of effort that we can recondition our mind and make the 80/20 Principle our modus operandi. When we make the 80/20 Principle a major part of our daily life, it cannot fail to help us achieve better results.

Let's use the 80/20 Principle to transform all areas of our life. Ignoring it will cost us our time and probably our dreams too.

It's that important.

Priority or lack thereof

Most problems are solvable if enough people get together and focus on them long enough and hard enough. Unfortunately, there are too many conflicting ideas and goals in this world. People have vested interests in pursuing certain goals, even if, in the grand scheme of things, those goals aren't the most important ones. That's why, rather than agreeing on key issues to solve, we all strive to solve different issues on our own.

When we attempt to solve thousands of different problems instead of directing our time, effort and creativity toward the few problems that matter most, we scatter our energy and accomplish little. It's far more effective to travel in one direction than to move in thousands of directions. But this would entail agreeing on the main issues to be solved.

The same goes for individuals. When we try to focus on too many projects at once, we spread ourselves too thin, scatter our energy, and end up achieving little.

Everybody wants a piece of the pie

We all want to show that we're solving problems, that we are being useful. Every organization on this planet must justify its existence. Every charity seeks to solve a problem and will attempt to raise as much money as they can, even if the specific problem isn't that important. However, once a dollar is used to solve an issue, it can't be used anywhere else.

In addition, once we're part of an organization, we'll convince ourselves that we're doing useful work, or perhaps even that the problem we're tackling is the most important issue the world is facing. After all, nobody wants to feel useless by working on unimportant tasks.

For these reasons (and others), solving major problems is tough.

Identifying what matters

How do we identify what truly matters? What criteria do we use to decide what issues are worth solving? How do we know when we're focusing on too many problems at the same time?

For instance:

- Should we focus on saving as many lives as possible?
- Should we focus on improving people's quality of life? If so, how should we measure progress?
- Should we prioritize human beings? If so, what about the environment or animals?

These are not easy questions.

Making the dominos fall

Many issues are interconnected. In other words, one issue that is solved can automatically solve other issues or make them easier to crack.

Here is one question we might consider:

If we could only solve a single core issue, which one would have the biggest positive impact on society?

Perhaps it is education. As young people become better educated, they will make better decisions, and be more likely to find a job and prosper.

Perhaps it is nutrition. By making sure children in poor countries have all the nutrients they need, we can solve the issue of malnourishment and enable them to develop properly. In turn, it may enhance their ability to study and improve their prospects

Perhaps it's health. By putting in place measures to fight malaria (for example), we would save many lives each year.

Ultimately, determining the few key issues to focus on is a challenging task. However, if we truly want to solve major issues, that's something we need to work on. Perhaps it starts at the individual level by deciding what main issues we're willing to allocate a little bit of our time and money to.

CONTROLLING OUR ATTENTION

Our attention is our most important asset.

What we do with it and how we direct it will determine our future.

Let's control our attention or someone else will.

16

ON FAILURE

Failure is feedback

Failure is when reality doesn't meet our expectations.

We hoped to pass an exam, but we "failed". We started a side hustle, but it didn't make any money. Or we went on a few dates, but it didn't go anywhere. Failure doesn't define us. We aren't "failures", it's just that we tried something that didn't quite work out.

Expectations vs. reality

A lot of the frustrations and disappointments we experience are the result of reality not matching our expectations.

If so, disappointment can be seen as a powerful tool for growth. It helps us keep aligned with reality. By acting in the real world, "failing", and being disappointed, we receive invaluable feedback. As we gather more feedback, we can adjust our actions so that, over time, our expectations meet reality.

Life is a never-ending process of alignment with reality. As we grow older and gain more experience, we take more effective action and achieve many of the results we desire.

Disappointment is a necessary evil.

Failure and success

The path toward our goals is never a straight line. It's made of ups and downs, and often consists of one step forward and two steps backward. What most people call "failure" is an integral part of the learning process that ultimately leads to success.

When mice are put in a maze and reach a dead end, they don't give up. They keep trying different paths until they find the exit. When babies try to walk, they don't beat themselves up each time they fall. They keep trying until they figure out how to walk.

There is no failure. There is only learning.

Once we realize that thinking in terms of "failure" is the wrong paradigm, we can increase our level of resilience and keep going. After all, we're not failing, we're merely gathering feedback.

Work of art or work in progress?

We can see ourselves as a work of art or as a work in progress. When we see ourselves as a work of art, we expect perfection. Everything that falls below our high expectations is a sign that we are failing. This leads us to feel discouraged, give up and, ironically, live far below our potential.

Conversely, when we see ourselves as a work in progress, we understand that we are flawed human beings and see "failures" as both inevitable and temporary. We know that life is a marathon, not a sprint, and we enjoy the process of improving over time.

We are a work in progress striving to become a work of art. Or perhaps we are a work of art in progress.

Feeling not good enough

Feelings of inadequacy are subjective. We can be a top performer in our field, or a wonderful person admired by many, and still experience a deep-seated fear of not being good enough. Alternatively, we may see ourselves as an "average" person, an untalented artist or even a downright bad person and barely experience such feelings.

We will never be good enough

If we accept the dichotomy of good enough vs. not good enough, we'll lose every time. Whatever line of work we're in, whatever creative endeavor we pursue, we could always be doing better—but we could also be doing worse. While our work might never be good enough, it can always be good enough *for now*.

Let's remember that *we're a work in progress* and so is everything we do. Our work is a representation of us at a specific moment in time, and we're imperfect human beings. Therefore, rather than trying to do flawless work, why not aim at doing the best we can today? Some days, our best will be quite good, other days it will suck.

But it's always good enough *for now*.

The rule of one

We need one life partner.

We need one successful business or career.

We need one hobby we love.

We need one skill we excel at.

We need one unique gift to give to the world.

Let's remember that no matter how many times we fail, no matter how many rejections we receive, for the things that matter most, we often need to be right just one time. We're one encounter away from meeting our life partner, one business idea away from being financially successful, and one skill away from achieving wild success.

In the end, we won't remember our countless failures, but we will definitely remember our few successes. For most things in life, we just need to be right once.

"Just one" thinking

When I write a book, my goal is to help just *one* person take *one* action or have *one* insight. If the book happens to sell a million copies, it's just one person multiplied by one million.

Similarly, if we're on a podcast with a million listeners, we're merely talking to one person times one million. If we deliver a speech to one thousand people, we're interacting with another human being times a thousand.

The point is, we're only ever talking to one person at a time. At least, it's how it feels to each person in the audience. And how it can start feeling to us with some practice.

Let's take pressure off our shoulders. We're merely having a conversation with another human being like us.

The joy of rejection

Rejection is the process of eliminating what is not good for us.

We want unsuitable partners to reject us fast.

We want bad prospects to leave.

We want disinterested people to unfollow us.

We want ghosting, missed sales and unfollows.

These are all welcome.

Weeding out what is bad for us is how we end up with what is good for us. Rejection is useful. Let's embrace it rather than shy away from it.

When quitting is good

Football coach, Vince Lombardi, once said, "Winners never quit, and quitters never win."

But is that so?

If we never quit on what doesn't work, how are we to discover what will work?

Resilience is essential. It's necessary for any kind of success. However, it's also responsible for many failures.

The truth is that, sometimes, we *must* quit.

Quitting is being human

Quitting is normal. We quit on things all the time. We abandon projects, leave friendships or change hobbies. Often, we quit because we don't want something badly enough. We aren't willing to sacrifice part of our lives to get it. This is perfectly rational. Our time is limited, and we should use it wisely. When it makes more sense for us to give up than to persevere, we usually quit. Put differently, our brains work as follows:

If reasons to give up are stronger than reasons to keep going, *then* quit.

If we want to keep going, we should consider ways to bring more excitement to what we do. Then, we should envision all the benefits we will gain from reaching our goals. If it still isn't compelling enough, perhaps it's time to move on to the next challenge.

Winners always quit

In truth, winners always quit (on what's *not* working for them). It leaves them room to focus on what matters most and persevere in the right direction.

We should probably quit more often and faster on what doesn't interest us, excite us or motivate us. By strategically quitting on the wrong things, we have a shot at "winning" on the right things (i.e., we have a better chance at uncovering what will work for us).

Why we persevere

Why do we persevere when we could give up? There are many factors in play. The main ones are:

- **Our level of conviction.** The more strongly we believe we can reach our goals, the more likely we are to persevere.
- **Our level of passion.** The more passionate we are about something, the more likely we are to persevere.
- **Feedback from the world.** The better the feedback we receive, the more likely we are to persevere. Positive feedback from multiple sources is usually a sign that we are on the right track.
- **Rate of improvement.** When we feel as though we're making progress toward our goals, we're more inclined to keep going.
- **Odds of success.** When the odds we will reach our goals are good, we feel more compelled to keep working at them.
- **Pain vs. pleasure.** When the cost of failure and/or the benefits of reaching our goals are high, persevering becomes easier.

These are the main factors that determine our level of resilience.

NOT KNOWING

Not knowing is the beginning of knowing.

Failing is the beginning of success.

Struggling is the beginning of finding solutions.

Wherever we are now is a steppingstone toward where we aspire to be.

17

ON EGO AND STATUS

Ego is the enemy of learning

Our ego stands in the way of:

- Asking for help,
- Accepting our mistakes,
- Being coachable,
- Thanking people, and
- Telling people we love them.

In many aspects, ego prevents us from learning. And learning is how we grow, discover more about ourselves and learn to live a meaningful life. As such, ego might be what stands between us and the fulfilling life we aspire to.

Ego and identity

Our ego is an attempt to create a fixed identity out of an ever-changing reality (and self). It's inherently limiting. In a sense, our ego is like a mental model. A mental model can be useful, but it can never encompass the full complexity of reality. Similarly, our ego can never encompass the full complexity of our self. That is why our willingness to accept the changing nature of reality and to update our identity over time is critical.

What clothes are we wearing?

Our identity is like the clothes we wear. We can change it based on our needs and aspirations. For example, we can wear the clothes of a passionate entrepreneur, a loving parent or an avid learner. And, over time, our identity will come to define us. Life is therefore an identity game. When we struggle to reach the desired results, it's often because we hold onto the wrong identity.

Let's choose the identity that serves us well. Let's wear the appropriate clothes for us right now.

Our desire to be liked

Some people claim they don't care what others think. But is it true? People who don't care what others think tend to be sociopaths or psychopaths. We probably don't want to be either.

In truth, we care about what people think—a lot. It's only our delusion and arrogance that makes us think we don't. Many of our actions are ruled by voices in our head—the voices of our parents, partners, bosses, colleagues, friends or neighbors. As I'm writing this, I care what my readers think, whether they will like what I say or whether I will come across as a jerk or a wise person.

Our goal should be to display a healthy level of caring—neither caring too much and being paralyzed by fear nor being outright sociopaths and harming others.

We care what people think and this is a good thing. It's a sign that we are sane.

Objectification

Objectification is turning a complex and ever-changing reality into fixed concepts that we can manipulate in our head.

For instance, everyone we see as being a means to an end is objectified. They become an object. A tool that can be used to help us reach our goals. By objectifying others, we forget the uniqueness and complexity of each individual.

We objectify concepts as well. That is, we can make certain concepts objects of worship or admiration. Put differently, we must hold the image of a concept in our mind so that we can think about it, admire it, play with it or build our identity around it.

Worshipping and objectifying are often an indication that we have ossified our thinking into fixed ideas. We have stopped seeing people as people. Or we have given objects or concepts more importance than they deserve. Let's be aware of what we're worshipping or objectifying. Then, let's ask ourselves if that's what we really want to worship.

What are our filters?

Whatever we deem important becomes a filter through which we assess the world around us. This filter ends up dictating our behavior and shaping our identity.

If we obsess over money, we'll give more weight to any action that can make us more money. We'll judge people based on the fatness of their bank account rather than the kindness of their heart. Every person we interact with will become a tool we can use to make more money.

If we obsess about power, we'll seek ways to dominate other people using manipulative techniques. Everyone that crosses our path will become a pawn that can be used to increase our power.

Therefore, let's pay attention to our filters. If we're constantly trying to get something from the world around us, perhaps we should change our filter and redirect our focus inward.

The cost of being wrong

When it costs us more to change our mind than to keep being wrong, we will usually choose the latter. We'd rather preserve our current "identity" than take the risk of losing our sense of self, become alienated from our peers or question our life choices.

In other words, most of us will choose maintaining the status quo over changing our beliefs. That's because we prioritize belonging over truth. Belonging is seen as essential to our survival while truth isn't.

The status game

We all seek to acquire status. We want to be seen as smart, spiritual or excellent at what we do. We aspire to be a great chess player, a professional athlete, or an accomplished salsa dancer. In other words, we have a strong need to find our place in society—to belong to a tribe.

Playing the status game seems to be an inevitability that comes with the disease called "being human". There is no cure. There is no escape.

Creating our unique status

While we all desire to find our place in society, not everyone can be a high executive, a Hollywood movie star, or a high-ranking politician. Fortunately, we can create our own status. We can each play the status game to win.

In truth, status is local and situational. That is, there is an almost unlimited amount of status to choose from. Ultimately, it's our responsibility to find (or create) the status that works for us. For instance, some people find great pride in excelling at their favorite online game. Others experience joy in being parents. Yet others enjoy being skilled public speakers.

We can think of having status as being "famous", admired and/or respected by a few people. Some of us strive to be loved by the entire world or reach levels of fame or wealth that are almost unattainable —and, if ever reached, never enough. As a result, they lose the status game and feel frustrated and unappreciated.

The point is, we all seek recognition in one way or another. But, to feel good about ourselves, we only need local status, not worldwide fame, to We merely need to be respected by some of our peers, whether they are other gamers, members of our dance club or coworkers.

The question we should ask ourselves is, "How can I win the status game in a way that makes sense to me?"

Criticism, naysayers and haters

Let's not dismiss criticism because it is disingenuous, exaggerated or plainly hurtful. Criticism can contain a grain of truth. Once our anger, frustration or fear of inadequacy settles, let's look at the criticism objectively. There is often something to be learned.

18

ON MONEY

Our relationship with money

Money is many things to many people. While money may seem like an abstract concept, all of us have an intimate relationship with it. We may love it. Or we may see ourselves as above it. But money leaves no one indifferent.

Money and time

Money can be seen as stored time. By accumulating money, we increase our stock of time. We can then invest that time in whatever way we please. We can use it to look for another job, start a business, focus on our hobbies or hang out with our loved ones. With more time, we have far more options in life.

Money as a communication tool

The way we make, spend and perceive money reveals a great deal about our character and values.

Let's try to have a healthy relationship with money by seeing it as a tool for exchanging values and expressing ourselves. Let's seek to make money in a way that feels good to us. Finally, let's spend it in a way that aligns with what matters most to us. This is far from an easy task, but it's worth trying.

Ultimately, the way we make and spend money is more important than how much of it we make or spend.

Money as an extension of ourselves

We can use money to express ourselves, broadcast our values and increase our impact. Or we can let it control us, live in fear of running out of it or become greedy.

Money is a wonderful servant, but a terrible master.

The best way to make money

People often ask, "What's the best way to make money?"

It's the wrong question.

Money isn't a magical thing that grows on trees. As intangible as it may seem, money comes from something very tangible—the blood, sweat and tears of anyone who decides to buy our products or services.

In other words, making money involves convincing people to give us a part of their scarcest resources—i.e., their time (which they used to make money). Consequently, the question we should ask ourselves isn't, "What's the best way to make money?" but, "Why should people part with their hard-earned money and give it to us?"

We can make a lot of money. But for that, we must give people something that, in their eyes, has more value than the price they paid.

It's simple math.

Adding value

Here is one simple question that, if we keep in the back of our mind, will enable us to do well financially over time:

How can I create more value?

If we spend the coming years relentlessly thinking of ways to add value through our products and services (and to people around us in general), we will likely make more money than we otherwise would have.

Now, how can we add value?

Adding value means making other people's lives better by:

- Solving some of their problems,
- Saving them time,
- Making them more money,
- Entertaining them, or
- Doing all the above.

That's because people want fewer problems, more time, more money and/or more joy in their lives.

Putting yourself in other people's shoes

The best way to add value is to practice putting ourselves in other people's shoes. When we truly desire to be helpful, we eventually will be. When our actions and decisions are taken in the interest of our clients or customers, they will feel it.

Worshipping money

Many people, especially younger generations, idolize influencers, celebrities, movie stars or tech billionaires. Wealthy people are often given a free pass just because they have money. But being wealthy doesn't excuse bad behavior. We're probably better off judging people by their strength of character than by the size of their bank account.

Scarcity vs. abundance

When we focus solely on saving and accumulating money, we tend to bury our talents and skills rather than use them to create value for society. We invest our money in things we have no control over (stock market, bonds or art) instead of investing it in what we have control over (our skills, talents and passions).

Instead of living a wealthy life *today* by using our resources to grow and reach meaningful goals, we live a life of scarcity by seeking to accumulate more money that we might enjoy *someday*.

Now, I'm not saying that we shouldn't save or invest, we definitely should. What I mean is that, when possible, we should practice using money as a tool for personal growth, and as a means to express our talents, skills and serve others, and not merely as something to be hoarded forever.

The point of having money

When we lack money, we think about it all day long. The point of making money is so that we don't have to think about it. People who become wealthy often forget that. They seek to make more and more money. In other words, they operate under the same system that governed them before—one of scarcity and fear.

Perhaps true wealth is when we don't think about money at all.

Spending money

Our present is always more valuable than our future, because the present moment is guaranteed while the future isn't.

If we keep accumulating money and unexpectedly die, we will have missed many opportunities to use our money in the present to create wonderful memories and have amazing experiences.

At the same time, we must remember that someday, our future will become our present. If we spend all our money now, we may struggle to pay future bills or we may have to lower our standard of living later in life.

Therefore, we must strike a healthy balance between enjoying our money now and investing it for the future.

Money and problems

Having money solves but also reveals problems. So long as our eyes are on being successful and making money, we have a clear goal to strive for. This goal can monopolize our attention and often give us purpose. However, if we ever reach a point where we make more money than we can spend, suddenly we must face all the issues we thought money would solve. For instance, we may realize that money doesn't bring us the sense of fulfilment we expected, solve our relationship issues, eliminate our feelings of inadequacy or alleviate our anxiety. In addition, we may also need to solve "new" problems we had buried for a long time.

As such, money is an interesting tool for personal growth. It can enable us to acquire all the material things and experiences we wanted (or thought we did), but it can also shed light on the problems left after we've done that.

Perhaps we can say that money reveals part of ourselves that we either didn't know were there or that we didn't want to deal with.

Money > time > energy > attention

Many of us think like this:

Money > time > energy > attention

That is, we value money more than time, time more than energy and energy more than attention.

First, we see money as being more important than time. As a result, we're willing to sacrifice our time for money.

Then, we fail to realize that our level of energy matters more than time or money. Therefore, we neglect to take care of our health to increase our energy level.

Finally, we exert little control over our attention. Where our attention goes is merely an afterthought—and we're mostly running on autopilot during the day.

But we have it backward. Instead, we should focus on the following:

Attention > energy > time > money

Our attention is more important than our energy level, our energy level matters more than our time and our time is more valuable than money.

This is because what we focus on (*attention*) dictates what we channel our *energy* toward, which determines how well we use our *time*, which, ultimately, impacts the amount of *money* we can generate.

Our attention is our superpower. When we direct it toward meaningful goals we really care about, we can do extraordinary things.

19

ON INDEPENDENT THINKING

Why smart people do stupid things

Intelligence doesn't protect us against stupidity.

It's not just unintelligent people who believe in wild conspiracies, join cults or say irrational things. Smart people do that too. They are as good as—if not better than—anyone else at convincing themselves that they are right. After all, they're masters at winning arguments. They know how to identify flaws in people's reasoning and will find effective ways to strengthen their own beliefs.

Humans are highly skilled at pattern recognition. Historically, being able to connect the dots is what allows us to survive. We would rather mistake a piece of wood for a snake than the other way around. Better safe than sorry.

Intelligent people excel at finding patterns. As a result, they sometimes connect too many dots (i.e., perceive patterns where none exist). Because they are smart, they can easily find pieces of information to strengthen their narrative. When you add to that the arrogance of thinking they're smarter than others, they have the potential to believe in almost anything.

The point is intelligence is simply not a protection against inaccurate thinking. We must always stay humble and open-minded.

Staying within our circle of competence

We give more weight to the opinion of people we like. And we do so even when they venture beyond their domain of expertise. But our favorite actor isn't a geopolitical expert. Nor is our favorite philosopher an economist, or our favorite influencer a professional investor. The point is, being a public figure doesn't mean that these people should have an opinion about anything and everything. And, when they do, we should give them far less credit than they deserve.

After all, most experts in their field can occasionally be wrong. Subject experts often disagree with each other. So why should we give much credit (if any) to non-experts?

Wanting others to be like us

One of our biggest biases is to think people should be just like us. It results from our inability to put ourselves in someone else's shoes. After all, there is only so much we can know about people's inner world.

We believe others have the same strengths or weaknesses we have. We believe they like or should like the same things we do. We believe they dress poorly when they don't dress like us. We believe they're misguided when they don't have the same religion as us. We think they are bad people when they have different political orientations than us.

But what sort of world would we be living in if everybody wore the same clothes, acted the same way or held the same beliefs as us?

Considering the level of self-delusion all of us are prone to experience at some point in our lives, we don't want others to be like us. We want people to hold different opinions so that we can talk each other out of our self-delusions, which are almost limitless.

We're all endangered when some people believe they know the truth, think they are right and want everybody else to agree with them.

Others aren't exactly like us—and they shouldn't be.

Going astray in life

Human beings like to turn everything into a movement—religions, political or economic ideas, philosophical schools and so on. As we join various movements, they soon become part of our identity.

Now, how can we protect ourselves? How can we find what's true? Fortunately, we have a few tools that may come in handy:

- **Humility.** Staying humble enables us to recognize how little we know and to self-reflect, learn and change direction as needed.
- *Self-awareness.* Cultivating more self-awareness helps us realize when we have gone astray.
- **Curiosity.** Being curious leads us to inquire continuously regarding what is true and what isn't.
- **Critical thinking.** Refining our ability to think helps us defend against various cognitive biases and helps us make wise decisions.

We *will* go astray.

The question is, for how long?

Repetition, familiarity and culture

Repetition and familiarity create the foundation on which cultures are built. What is a culture if not a set of commonly accepted practices and rules we rely on to coexist (relatively) peacefully?

We need a common ground on which to build a culture. In a hypothetical world where nobody lives in the same place more than one day, it would be impossible to build any culture. Put differently, culture requires time and space. The same people need to stay at the same place for long enough for culture to emerge. There needs to be "conformity" of practices, rules and thoughts over time. The way we greet each other, what we eat, how we behave in public or what kind of buildings we erect constitute part of a culture.

How do we develop critical thinking when, by definition, the culture we were born in inevitably hinders this to some extent?

That's a difficult question. Critical thinking seems to go against our natural tendency—and probably biological need—to gather and organize ourselves around a set of commonly accepted beliefs.

Let's keep that in mind as we try to become independent thinkers.

The enemies of critical thinking

Clichés, proverbs, quotes, propaganda or accepted "truths".

These are all signs that we aren't thinking.

As we age, we gradually stop thinking. We repeat clichés we've heard countless times. We quote smart people without questioning the truth of their words. We believe what we've been told repeatedly. And what we see as common sense is sometimes nonsense.

That's because it's easier to keep believing what we already believe than to update our beliefs, which would entail rewiring our brain. This is just too much work.

For many of us, the path of least resistance is simply to keep believing in what we already consider as true—for better or for worse.

The danger of clichés

It's the journey, not the destination. Believe in yourself. Never give up. Your health is your wealth. Knowledge is power. Happiness starts within.

All these expressions contain powerful truths. But how many of us truly understand them and live by them?

Sadly, we often dismiss clichés, failing to realize the truth they're pointing to. The more we hear them, the more they lose their substance. Clichés—though they may contain kernels of truth—end up being the enemy of truth. They become what prevents us from having the direct experience required to internalize the wisdom they contain.

That's why my editor highlights any clichés in my manuscript. Clichés fail to catch the reader's attention; they don't land. Instead of helping us make a point, they weaken it. Upon hearing a cliché, people's immediate reaction is "I already know that". Then, they move on to the next point.

"I already know that"

As our mind becomes filled with clichés, we become increasingly disconnected from reality. We "know" everything about everything, yet we have little success to show for ourselves. And because we seem to "know" so much, nothing is new to us.

If we fail to achieve the results we want in life, it might be because we have too many unquestioned clichés in our head. Put differently, we have too much intellectual knowledge, but not enough actual experience and internalized wisdom.

Intellectual knowledge vs. internalized wisdom

Our level of success (and impact) in the real world is largely proportionate to our ratio of internalized wisdom to intellectual knowledge. The higher the ratio, the better.

Internalized wisdom is what we understand at a deeper level through direct experience. It's true knowledge acquired through tangible actions and thoughtful reflection.

Intellectual knowledge is what we *think* we know because we read a book about it, watched a documentary or passed an exam. It's the junk food of knowledge. For instance, it is:

- The person who knows everything about entrepreneurship but has never built a successful business,
- The self-help addict who read dozens of books, but whose life remains the same, and
- The intellectual who has never run a business but tells everybody how the economy should work.

What we believe we know (but don't) is often what leads us to be stuck. We can't learn anything new when we think we already know everything. Therefore, let's question how much we know about a specific topic. Let's seek to learn things from direct experience, not merely intellectually.

Black-and-white thinking

Rules, guidelines, frameworks, mental models.

These can be useful in helping us navigate life, but the truth is, few rules, guidelines, frameworks or mental models work for everyone all the time. For instance:

- Some people tell us to be more confident. Meanwhile, others suggest that we should finish the task in front of us, whether we feel confident or not.
- Some people recommend to say "yes" to every opportunity. Others advise us to say "no" to almost everything and focus on our priorities.
- Some people suggest that, to make more money, we should have specific things we want to buy as rewards to motivate us. Meanwhile, there are frugal people making millions, who barely touch their money.

There is no magic answer. Every situation is different.

Having several mental models, principles and rules to choose from will help us, but picking the right ones based on our personal situation will be by far the hardest part.

Breaking the rules

Rules are here to guide us, protect us and make it easier for us to live together, but we can sometimes forget why they exist in the first place and what they can and can't do for us.

For instance, one rule is to wait before crossing the road when the traffic light is red. Teaching kids to respect that rule is useful. However, when we forget to look at the oncoming traffic and look only at the traffic light, we make it a rigid rule instead of a useful guideline. In doing so, we replace independent thinking with the blind following of rules. One day, a driver may be distracted and go through a red light. And if we merely look at the light, we might find ourselves in imminent danger.

This is merely one example of obsessing over rules while forgetting the underlying principles. The point is this. Rules can't replace personal responsibility. They aren't an excuse to throw away the need to think for ourselves.

Transcending paradigms

Paradigms can be useful to help us make sense of the world. They can enable us to see problems in different ways and shift our perspective, but a paradigm is merely a data point, not a principle to follow to the letter.

Ideologies, political ideas, religious cults or movements such as minimalism or FIRE (Financial Independence, Retired Early) are merely tools to help us think and deepen our understanding of ourselves and the world.

But, as human beings, we tend to see any movement or ideology as an end rather than as a means. Our desire to belong to a certain community can be so strong that we may be willing to abandon our ability to think. Perhaps it's because, for many of us, belonging to something is more important than freedom. In truth, reality is complex. By exposing ourselves to countless paradigms, and by learning to transcend them—i.e., to see beyond them—we can become well-rounded human beings.

Some people

Some people should work more, others less.

Some people should speak up, others be quiet.

Some people should exercise more, others less.

Some people should save more, others spend more.

Some people should be more ambitious, others less ambitious.

There is no one-size-fits-all solution. People who think otherwise have abandoned critical thinking a long time ago. Rules are merely guidelines. Mental models are merely useful tools. Pieces of advice are merely data points. Ultimately, we must think for ourselves. We must be our own scientists and figure out what works best for us. No one else can do that for us.

Asking the right questions

The quality of the questions we ask ourselves largely determines the quality of our life. Therefore, we should try to ask ourselves better questions so that we can move closer to the life we desire. Here are some examples of poorly framed questions followed by more effective ones.

How can I find the right partner?

Better question: What kind of person do I need to be to attract my ideal partner?

How can I achieve my goals?

Better question: How can I become the kind of person who inevitably achieves my goals?

How can I make more money?

Better question: How can I create so much value that I have no choice but to become wealthy?

How can I retire early?

Better question: How can I live my life in such a way that I never have to (or want to) retire?

How can I change the world?

Better question: How can I understand myself and the world better so that each of my actions is impactful?

In many aspects, we don't attract what we want, we attract who we are. The ultimate question then is:

Who do we need to be if we want to attract the life we dream of?

Who will save us?

No guru can save us.

Nobody can answer all our questions.

No one can tell us how to live our lives.

Confidence: the good, the bad and the ugly

Life is uncertain, we often feel lost, and we're looking for the next person to tell us how to live our lives. We want to believe that someone else has the answers to our questions. We want someone to make decisions for us instead of having to take responsibility for our actions.

This is why confidence can be both powerful and dangerous. Throughout history there has been no lack of confident people. Hitler was confident in his ability to execute his vision, and he convinced millions of people to follow him. Religious fanatics commit acts of terrorism. They certainly don't lack confidence either.

Confidence can be useful to a certain point, but when people start telling us they know all the answers and that we should follow them, we should be wary.

Cultivating our personal philosophy

We can't blindly follow a cult, ideology, or trend. Doing this would rob us of our ability to think critically, and it would prevent us from implementing the philosophy that will work for us. Instead, we must establish our own philosophy. Doing so will enable us to express ourselves more authentically, and it will create more meaning in our lives.

To cultivate our personal philosophy, we must continually reflect on what we learn and are exposed to. Self-reflection is how we protect ourselves against other people's shared hallucinations as well as our own delusions. And it will help us figure out the values we want to live by and the kind of person we want to be.

Being our own brand

In many aspects, we are our own brand. Everything we do reflects who we are, what we like or what we value.

What we call fashion is a good illustration of our personal brand. People mistakenly believe that the logos on their clothes or how much they pay for them is what constitutes the brand. However, in truth, *we* are the brand. The quality of the clothes we wear, our choice of colors, and the way we assemble them to look a certain way is what constitutes our unique brand.

We are the brand—and we use clothes to make us more of who we are or of who we aspire to be.

If so, we can argue that logos, especially ostentatious ones, are an attempt to escape from our responsibility of being ourselves—or figuring out who we are. Sure, we can wear a bunch of clothes from luxury brands and make a clear statement that we have "money" or that we are cool. But neither having money nor trying to be trendy is who we are.

That isn't to say we should never buy clothes from expensive brands. They can be a great way to celebrate special occasions, make memorable gifts or enhance our overall look. But let's make sure we don't lose our personality in the process.

Let's look at another metaphor.

We can choose to write a book by merely assembling quotes from other people. But, in doing so, how much of our personality would shine through that book? The quotes will become more important than what we have to say. Or, in fashion terms, the logos become more important than the brand (i.e., us).

The same principle goes for any other aspect of our lives. We can work for someone else, but it doesn't mean we should forget about our own unique strengths, talents, personality and centers of interest.

The point is, we are always the brand. Our mission in life might be to figure out ways to:

- Find out who we are, and
- Find ways to express our uniqueness in various areas of our lives.

Agreeing with people

We'll never agree 100% with anyone. If we need to agree with everything someone else says before being their friends, we'll never have any friends. In fact, we probably don't even agree with many of the things we used to believe nor approve of some of our past actions or behaviors. How can we expect to agree with someone else all the time?

Society consists of people who disagree with each other yet agree to debate respectfully and live together peacefully.

We will never agree with anyone 100%—and we shouldn't.

The limit to knowing others

If we're a man, we'll never truly understand what it feels like to be a woman, and vice versa.

If we're born in America, we'll never understand what it means to be born in China.

If we belong to the main ethnic group in our country, we'll never understand what it feels like to be part of an ethnic minority.

The way we experience the world is inevitably tainted by the country we were born in, how our parents raised us, whether we are a man or a woman, our genes, any past traumas, as well as countless other factors. Trying to put ourselves in someone else's shoes is therefore one of the hardest things to do.

Perhaps one of the points in life is to seek to understand others better, to observe more, read more and try to be exposed to as many perspectives as possible so that we can grasp the full picture a little better.

We can never truly know anyone.

But we can try.

Rationality vs. spirituality

We may take pleasure in being the "rational" ones. We may express disdain and disgust for anything, or anyone, associated with spirituality. Whether we realize it or not, we see ourselves as better than others. We know the "truth" while others are delusional. The problem is that, by acting in this way, we risk separating ourselves from fundamental values such as faith, reverence or humility.

By seeing ourselves as the ones in charge, we forget there is something bigger than ourselves, and that there are things we will never understand. We lose the art of letting go and surrendering.

The bottom line is, we may think that what others believe is stupid, but it doesn't mean we can't or shouldn't explore spirituality. Spirituality is something intimate. The way we relate to the universe is deeply personal. What others believe or don't believe shouldn't get in the way of us exploring our relationship with God, the divine, the universe or whatever we choose to call it.

Now, it is also true that many so-called religious people feel superior for being "more" religious than their neighbor, or for believing in the "right" God, but we don't have to be like them. We can explore spirituality in our own way.

Let's try to remain humble, grateful and curious about the world.

Seeking truth

We say we want the truth, but is that so? Do we really want to know what people around us think of us? Are we ready to find out all the things they don't like about us? Are we willing to change our political or religious beliefs completely if, upon seeking truth, we realize we might have been on the wrong path?

Often, we don't seek what is true, we merely seek what's useful to us or what increases our level of happiness. Perhaps this is part of being human.

Selling shovels

During the gold rush, people selling shovels made the most money with minimum risk involved. Today's sellers of shovels are people such as business coaches, finance Youtubers and real estate gurus.

Many "business" coaches build their businesses by trying to tell us how to run ours.

Most finance YouTubers tell us how to get rich (a few decades from now) by investing in stocks. But the way *they* grew rich is usually through YouTube ads revenue, paid partnerships or by selling courses.

And many real estate gurus make most of their money from selling expensive courses while their success as real estate investors is often dubious at best.

Follow this simple rule: *learn from people who have achieved the results you want.*

- Learn how to create a business from people who have built multiple successful businesses in the same niche as you (if possible).
- Learn how to become wealthy from people who teach you how *they* became rich.
- Learn real estate from people who own tons of real estate.

The hardest part is to find good role models. Successful people often have no incentive or no time to teach us what they know. They don't need our money. They have nothing to sell us. They're busy focusing on what they're good at.

Let's listen to people who are getting results, not people who are simply after our money.

20

ON BUILDING AN ANTIFRAGILE LIFE

Life is inherently risky and unpredictable. While we do not have complete control over our lives, we can learn to mitigate risks to increase our chances of being happy and successful.

To reuse Nassim Taleb's famous concept in a somewhat different context, we can strive to build an "antifragile" life—i.e., become more resilient. In this section, let's see how we can do so in various areas of life.

Mindset

Although "mindset" is a word that might have been overused, it doesn't make it less important. The way we think has a massive impact on the quality of our life. A positive outlook on life and the ability to frame events in a constructive way, makes us more antifragile, and it dramatically increases the odds that we will reach our goals.

Let's see what we can do specifically to build a positive mindset that serves us.

Learning how to learn

One thing we can be sure of is that the future will require us to adapt and learn new skills. Therefore, the most valuable skill we can develop to become more resilient is learning how to learn. This is referred to as meta-learning.

In short, being an exceptional learner makes us antifragile. It starts by adopting the mindset that we can learn almost any skill we need to reach almost any goal we might have.

The joy of learning

Learning is one of the greatest joys in life. We'll never understand much about the world, but we can rejoice in learning something new each day.

Continuously improving

The better we become, the more doors open to us. We cannot choose our immediate circumstances, but we can choose to become better in many ways—i.e., a more attentive listener, a refined thinker, an eloquent speaker, a skilled leader and so on. Improving ourselves can not only be an enjoyable process, but it can also make us even more antifragile.

A mindset of continuous improvement is key to reaching any of our goals.

Seeing problems as opportunities

We can choose to perceive our problems as opportunities to overcome weaknesses, eliminate blind spots, create better systems or learn about ourselves (our strengths, weaknesses, abilities or centers of interest). When we do so, each problem we face becomes a way for us to improve and become more antifragile. In other words, our challenges enable us to develop new tools, frameworks, and mental models to help us solve future problems.

In summary, to build a more antifragile mindset, let's:

- Realize that we can learn any skill we need to reach any goal we have,
- Focus on continuous improvement, and
- See any problem as an opportunity to grow and learn more about ourselves.

Emotional state

Our emotional state is one of the most important components of our life. How much of life can we enjoy when we're unhappy, stressed or dissatisfied?

Let's see what we can do to help us become emotionally more antifragile.

Nurturing close relationships

One of the greatest predictors of fulfilment and longevity is the strength of our social circle. And it doesn't matter whether we're extroverted or introverted. Some people need more time alone, but for our well-being, we all need to spend time around people.

Diversifying our network

When we are being overly dependent on one person for our emotional well-being and social connection, we're at risk of being left alone and lonely if the relationship goes south. As Arthur C. Brooks wrote in *From Strength to Strength*, "Having your spouse or partner as your one and only close friend is imprudent, like having a radically undiversified portfolio. If something goes wrong in your marriage, you can be left single *and* without friends."

By having several close friends, belonging to different social groups (church, sports clubs, associations, et cetera), having a significant other and maintaining good relationships with family members, we can become emotionally more secure (antifragile).

In other words, we should diversify our investment in our relationships.

Practicing gratitude

We can't always get everything we want, but we can always learn to appreciate what we already have. When we appreciate what we have, we are less likely to fall prey to negative emotions.

Celebrating our wins

When we focus on perfection, we risk never feeling good enough. On the other hand, when we focus on progress, we can take pride in all the small wins we accumulate day after day. Celebrating our wins is another tool for becoming emotionally antifragile.

Avoiding comparison

We have our own issues to solve and our own paths to walk. The best we can do is to strive to become a little better each year.

Let's avoid comparing ourselves to others. Instead, let's embrace our own path and fight our own battles—and let others do the same.

Cultivating self-compassion

Self-compassion is a safety net for our emotional well-being. Furthermore, self-criticism is a sure way to feel bad about ourselves.

Self-criticism breaks us while self-compassion enables us to bend and bounce back. With a healthy dose of self-compassion, like a reed, we bend yet never break. We become more resilient. We become antifragile.

Having compelling goals

Most of us aren't lazy, we merely lack exciting goals to strive for. By having compelling goals that we move toward each day, we will stay motivated and avoid being overwhelmed by negative emotions.

Staying inspired

We have a bias toward negativity. To become emotionally more antifragile, we must reverse this trend and infuse more positivity into our lives daily.

Let's expose ourselves to positive content while avoiding negativity when it's unnecessary. Let uplifting books, inspiring podcasts and educational videos be our friends.

Creating a strategy to climb out of a slump

It's easier to avoid a fall into negative emotions than to climb out of them. As such, it's worth creating a specific plan to help us snap out of a negative state before things deteriorate.

The sooner we can notice when we're feeling sad, anxious or a little depressed, the faster we can act. Self-awareness is the first step. The more we know ourselves, the better we can identify what could help us revert to a more positive state.

Meditation, self-compassion, gratitude, exercise and chatting with friends are some of the tools we can use to improve our emotional state and become more resilient.

Let's craft our strategy. Then, let's refine it over time.

Managing pain and pleasure effectively

Life is about contrast. By actively choosing the pain we want to experience, we can increase our level of resilience. If we refuse to choose the pain we want, we'll often experience pain that we do not want.

Cold swimming, sauna, or challenging workouts are activities that may scare us a little, but they are positive stresses to put on our body and mind. Also, they make us more resilient.

To sum up, to become emotionally more antifragile, let's:

- Nurture close relationships,
- Diversify our network of friends,
- Practice gratitude,
- Celebrate our wins,
- Avoid comparison,
- Set compelling goals,
- Stay inspired,

- Develop strategies to pick ourselves up, and
- Learn to manage pain and pleasure effectively.

Physical health

Our physical health will deteriorate as we age but there are a few things we can do to help us remain healthy, or at least, increase the odds that we do.

Prevention over cure

Curing an illness is always more expensive, painful and emotionally challenging than preventing it. Not to mention, it's less certain.

Let's strive to prevent diseases years before they happen. We can do so by exercising consistently, eating healthily and doing blood work on a regular basis. We should also seek to identify our biggest health risks based on our family history and genetic predisposition. Then, let's do whatever we can to reduce those risks.

Working out

Exercising offers many benefits. Therefore, let's go to the gym, walk, stretch, play sports and so on. In short, let's do whatever we can to stay active every day for the rest of our life. This will increase both our mental and physical health. It will make us more antifragile.

Many issues result from us not moving enough. What we fail to use, starts dying. Let's make sure we're using our body each day and staying active.

In summary, to improve our physical health and become more resilient, let's:

- Identify our biggest risks by doing blood work and looking at our family history,
- Seek to prevent diseases before they happen, and
- Make sure we work out on a regular basis.

Career

To become antifragile in our career, one key element is to choose financial confidence over financial freedom.

By focusing too much on *financial freedom*, we risk obsessing over how much money we have in our bank account. We may become anxious every time we lose money or may live in fear of losing it all.

On the other hand, by focusing on building *financial confidence*, we can reduce such anxiety. Being financially confident means knowing that we can always make money regardless of our external situation. At least, we feel confident in our ability to do so.

The ultimate goal is building the confidence that we can make money in almost any situation thanks to the skills we've developed, experiences we've acquired, network we've built or the mindset we've cultivated over the years. Now, here is what we can do to build stronger financial confidence:

Learning useful skills. Whether we're an employee or a business owner, we're always the CEO of our own life—and career. The more skills we possess, the more opportunities we have to earn promotions or switch careers as needed.

Useful skills will vary from person to person, but some examples might be:

- **Sales skills.** We're selling all the time—and we are selling ourselves during job interviews or when seeking a promotion.
- **Language skills.** Speaking one foreign language fluently can open the door to a new market and countless opportunities.
- **Certifications.** Having multiple certifications required in a specific industry may make us more valuable in the marketplace.

These are just a few examples.

Whatever can help us increase our financial confidence is useful.

Being future-oriented

The best way to protect ourselves against an uncertain future is to prepare for it. We do this by embracing the future rather than fighting against it. Here are a few things we can do:

- **Focusing on growing industries.** It's easier to be successful when we're on a rocket ship than on a sinking boat.
- **Learning universal skills.** We want to acquire skills that enable us to land a job in most countries. Communication skills are probably among the most important ones. Let's remember that most money made in this world comes from interacting with customers. Communication skills include languages, writing skills or public speaking skills, but also programming (computer language). The better communicators we are, the more antifragile we become.
- **Acquiring skills that are in high demand.** Some skills are in greater demand than others. For instance, engineers will seldom have trouble finding a job. The same can probably be said for doctors, nurses or experienced salespeople.
- **Building antifragile streams of income.** Expensive or discretionary products are harder to sell than inexpensive ones. And having a physical store is less antifragile than selling online. Whenever possible, we should strive to create streams of income that will not stop no matter what happens.

As we seek to implement some or all of these things, we will become more antifragile over time and less worried about the future.

In summary, to become more resilient in our career, let's seek to become more financially confident by:

- Learning useful skills,
- Focusing on growing industries, and
- Building antifragile income streams.

Finance

To protect our finances and build/preserve our financial health, here are a few things we can do:

- **Building multiple streams of income.** The more streams of income we have, the more financially resilient we become. For instance, an employee can lose their job overnight and be left with nothing. But someone who, in addition to a 9-to-5 job, has a side hustle that brings in a few thousand dollars a month will be better off during tough times.
- **Saving money.** Money represents the time and energy we spend working. When we save money, we store that time and energy for later use, which gives us more options and makes us more resilient. If we lose our job, we have more time to look for another one. If we're building a business, we can focus on it for longer before running out of money. If we have an emergency, we can deal with it without jeopardizing our financial situation.
- **Having multiple bank accounts in different countries.** Once we have a substantial amount of money, we should spread it over multiple bank accounts and/or investment platforms. We can never know what will happen to a certain bank or country. Even deposit insurance from a country is not guaranteed to work when that country faces an unpredictable crisis.
- **Diversifying our investments.** By having our money invested in different assets, we can protect ourselves against the risk of losing everything. We should do our research and invest in what we understand, whether it is stocks, real estate, arts, cryptocurrencies or watches—and diversify enough. If there is even the slightest chance that we might lose everything because of an economic crisis, a natural disaster or any other unpredictable event, we're not properly diversified.
- **Getting insurance.** We can't afford not to be insured against any risk that could wreak havoc in our life. Missing a flight

might not be a big deal, but getting into a car accident, falling seriously sick while traveling or having our house burned down is a big deal and can ruin our life. We should get proper insurance for what matters most. We can't afford not to.

In short, to improve our finances and build our wealth, let's:

- Multiply our streams of income,
- Save money,
- Have multiple bank accounts in different countries,
- Diversify our investments, and
- Get proper insurance.

Eliminating points of failure

In our attempts to become more antifragile, there are many things that can wreak havoc. There are holes in our approach—and we may be oblivious to them. That's why we must look at single points of failure that could render all our efforts futile. To do so, we must answer the following questions:

- In what ways am I vulnerable right now?
- What major risks am I ignoring or being oblivious to?

Let's go over various areas of our life.

Mental health/emotional state

Is there one event that could impact our mental health? What could we do to protect it and maintain a positive emotional state?

Health

Is there one event that could destroy our health? What could we do to protect it and prevent future issues?

Career

Is there one event that could jeopardize our entire career? If we're employed, is there a risk we could lose our job? If we're self-employed or have our own business, what could jeopardize our business and/or lead us to lose most of our customers?

Finance

Is there one event that could put us in a dire financial situation? Are we overexposed to a certain asset? Is our mortgage too high? Do we have enough savings?

Insurance

Is there one event that our insurance doesn't cover and that could destroy our life? What could we do to protect ourselves against such an event?

Overall

What danger are we exposed to in our country or neighborhood?

To conclude, while the future can be unpredictable, we can do our best to protect ourselves against the biggest issues that might wreak havoc in our life. Once every few months, it's worth taking the time to assess the level of risk we're taking in various areas of our life so that we can make ourselves more resilient to unpredictable events.

The bottom line is this. Life is uncertain. This is why we must put in place strategies to help us become more antifragile regardless of external circumstances.

21

ON THE DANGER OF PERSONAL DEVELOPMENT

People drawn toward personal development have a certain personality. They are often ambitious and may feel underappreciated. They have a sense that there is more to life.

There's nothing wrong with that, as such.

The problem arises when we start turning personal development into some kind of religion. Then, it becomes an "us vs. them" dynamic. We're improving ourselves and they aren't. When we do this, we create a separation between us (the "self-aware") and others (the "unaware").

Let's briefly review some of the dangers of personal development.

Lack of compassion.

"It's their fault if they are where they are".

"They didn't work hard enough".

The more we take responsibility for our life, the harder it is to accept that others won't or can't. Personal development is often what we do when we're not struggling anymore for our day-to-day survival.

Unfortunately, many people don't have the emotional room or the means to think about improving themselves.

Let's not forget that.

Sense of superiority

Since we're working on ourselves, we're necessarily better than people who aren't, right? During our personal development journey, we can easily start feeling superior to others. We forget one of the most important qualities in life:

Humility.

Fear of negativity

Our desire to succeed leads us to stay away from negativity, sometimes to the extreme. When we see people who are struggling financially, emotionally or physically, we're afraid to become like them. We're scared that it will pollute our mind, negatively affect our mindset and make us more likely to fail.

As a result, feeling compassion toward others becomes harder. Perhaps, this is one of the many paradoxes of personal development.

Obsession with money

Personal development is difficult to measure. But money is easy to count. That's why money tends to become the proxy through which we measure our success. Making money means we are "adding value" to the world, which means we are successful, which means our personal development has borne fruit. Or, put differently, the more value we create for others, the more money we deserve to make—or so we believe.

As a result, making money starts taking precedence over everything else. The desire to make money leads some of us to do unethical things so that we can deliver more "value". It justifies shady business practices such as multi-level marketing, crypto "investments" or the purchase of fake followers.

However, in truth, making a lot of money isn't a sign that we're helping people. Otherwise, no scammers would ever be able to make millions. And we can doubt that drug dealers and human traffickers are adding much value to society.

Sometimes, instead of growing ourselves, we end up obsessing over growing our bank account. Instead of building our character, we're merely trying to build our wealth.

Cult-like thinking

Sadly, many self-help gurus behave like cult leaders. Under the influence of such "gurus", our genuine desire to improve, to be useful to others and to make a decent living turns into an obsession with money, success and power.

Perhaps the antidote is:

- Seeking to master our craft,
- Striving to be useful,
- Cultivating critical thinking,
- Becoming more self-aware,
- Focusing on building our character,
- Staying humble, and
- Never choosing money over our own conscience.

22

STATISTICS AND PREDICTIONS

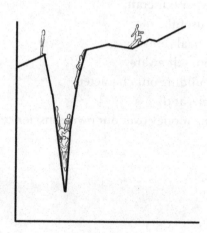

How to avoid becoming a statistic

We all have the ability to change our lives, often far more dramatically than we imagined. We can learn new skills, switch careers or improve our health. Or we can develop virtues such as courage, discipline or integrity. Yet, while, in theory, everybody can change, in practice, many people don't.

You likely have heard different versions of the sentence starting with: "Not everybody can..."

- Not everybody can be a millionaire.
- Not everybody can have a career they enjoy.
- Not everybody can be fit and healthy.

And from a statistical point of view, these statements are accurate.

The problem is that, thinking in terms of statistics may lead us to feel discouraged and prevent us from doing the work needed to reach our goals. While it is true that not everybody can, many people likely could. Many of us *could* make progress toward our goals and reach quite a few of them.

"Not everybody can" often becomes an excuse we use to justify why we don't have the life we desire. It often becomes synonymous with "I won't bother trying".

Let's face it. Statistics are real, but we don't have to become yet another statistic. There are specific things we can do to improve the odds of reaching our goals, whatever they may be.

The fallacy of statistics

Because 50% of marriages end in divorce doesn't mean we have a 50% chance of getting a divorce. There are things we can do to improve our odds. Because 48% of new businesses fail after five years doesn't mean our chance of success is equivalent to a coin flip. For instance, if we're a seasoned entrepreneur our chances of success improve.

Here is an even more interesting example. 94% of US fund managers perform worse than the S&P 500 over 20 years (the S&P 500 index tracks the stock performance of 500 of the largest companies listed on stock exchanges in the United States). Now, does it mean that, as individual investors, we also have a 94% chance of underperforming the S&P 500?

No. In fact, merely by putting our money in an index fund tracking the S&P 500 and leaving it there for 20 years, we'll outperform 94% of professional fund managers (assuming future trends follow past trends).

This shows how statistics can be misleading. And that's why we shouldn't let statistics run our lives. Instead, we should do whatever is in our power to stack the odds in our favor.

The bottom line is, statistics are useful. They provide us with a baseline and inform us of the likelihood of an event to happen. Let's use them to improve our odds, rather than seeing them as our destiny.

How to lie with statistics

Recently, as I was traveling to Italy, an employee at a butchery asked me whether it was true there were more women than men in Estonia (where I live). I replied that it was.

But later, when looking at the data, I found out that it was only true for people over 50. From age 0 to 50, there are more men than women in Estonia.

The moral of the story is that things aren't always as clear cut as they seem. And we can easily mislead people by using statistics in a way that tells an incomplete and disingenuous story.

Let's beware of statistics.

Why predictions suck

Let's be wary of anyone who makes predictions. The more bold and specific predictions someone makes, the more skeptical we should be.

For instance, if an "expert" predicts an economic crisis this year (like some do every year), we should probably stop listening. They likely don't have our best interests at heart, nor do they have a deep interest in truth. They may seek to generate buzz to grow their audience or try to sell us something. In any case, we should be careful.

Predicting an economic crisis, like many other things, is a fool's errand, or a fun game to play at best. We can try to assign probabilities to various scenarios, but even that is a wild guess. Therefore, the more confident someone sounds with their predictions, the less we should listen.

The point is, there is already too much bad data out there. Let's be selective over whom we listen to.

Looking for patterns

Something that occurs once is a mistake, something that occurs several times becomes a pattern.

- If someone is late once, it's a minor incident, but if they are late on multiple occasions, it becomes a pattern.
- If someone lies once, it might be a one-off, but if someone lies several times, it's probably a habit.
- If someone commits a petty crime once, it might be excusable under certain conditions, but if it happens repeatedly, we have a pattern.

When there is smoke there isn't always fire. But when there is smoke in multiple locations, there often is.

The asymmetry of information

When we don't know anything about a topic, we're easy to fool. When our dentist tells us we have a cavity, or the mechanic points out an issue with our car, we have little choice but to believe them.

Similarly, when we read about a topic we know little about, we tend to believe the journalist who wrote the piece. But, when we're knowledgeable, we can immediately tell if they have their facts wrong —and they often do.

Try it for yourself. Take any topic you consider yourself an expert in. Then, see how often the news distorts the facts, oversimplifies things or blatantly attempts to manipulate people to push an agenda.

Now, if they can be so wrong about the few topics we know about, how likely are they to be wrong about other topics we know little about?

23

ON HUMAN NATURE

The human experience

Humans are imperfect. Being human means falling short. It's feeling jealous, frustrated and hopeless at times. It's experiencing all kinds of unpleasant and vile thoughts we wish we didn't have. It's repeatedly failing to reach our goals. And, sometimes, it's hating ourselves.

None of these are problems, though.

The issue is that we fight against the reality of our existence. We deny ourselves our inalienable right to have the human experience we came to earth for. We reject our rights to be imperfect, to have shadows, to make mistakes. In doing so, we enslave ourselves in a world of constant suffering where our expectations are crushed over and over, as they are bound to be.

Perhaps we should remind ourselves that there is nothing wrong with being a human being and having a human experience—or our suffering will never cease.

Self-compassion

Self-compassion is the humble recognition that we're imperfect human beings and that we should treat ourselves as such. It's forgiving and encouraging ourselves to do the best we can with what we have.

Self-compassion is how we continually encourage ourselves on our personal growth journey. Ultimately, it's what enables us to feel better and achieve more of what matters to us.

Looking for the "pause" button

Just because we have had good habits for thirty years doesn't mean we can stop doing what we were doing. Life is about what we do each day. It's a never-ending process.

- A good marriage is the result of how we interact with our spouse each day, not how much we loved them when we said "yes" at the altar.
- Good mental and physical health is the result of daily habits such as meditating, practicing gratitude or working out.
- A thriving business is the result of ongoing marketing and continuous improvement of our products or services.

We can never stop. We can't pause and keep everything as it is during the rare moment when we feel fulfilled and at peace.

In life, there is no "pause" button.

Grow or die

In nature, nothing ever remains stable. The same goes for human beings and human-related activities.

Many of us complain that businesses are greedy and only care about getting bigger and making more profits. But could it be any different? The moment a CEO decides, consciously or unconsciously, to stop growing the business they oversee, the company starts dying. People stop giving their best and the top employees may even move to another company.

A company with thousands of employees has no choice but to grow. Its employees depend on the company's survival for their survival and for the survival of their family. Over a long enough time, any company will disappear, and its employees will have to find other jobs. But it won't be without a fight. The company will try to stay alive for as long as it can.

No company, country or empire can grow forever. Eventually, it will decay. That's just the cycle of life. Growth and death are inevitable. Similarly, as humans, we either grow or die. We sharpen the skills we focus on. We strengthen the relationships we put the effort into. We grow the muscles we train. Conversely, whatever we fail to use starts to die. Therefore, let's focus on the things that matter most to us so that we can grow in a meaningful way. And let everything else wither and die.

Fear vs. love

At any point in time, we act either out of fear or out of love. To explain, when we act out of fear, we're trying to get something out of people, and when we act out of love we're trying to give something to people. Fear leads us to seek attention, fame, money or power. Love leads us to give our time, money, creativity or attention to the world.

Let's start paying attention and identifying when we're acting out of fear and when we're acting out of love.

Silence

Being silent isn't a passive act. It's a deliberate choice to allow whatever may come—insights, feelings, intuition, et cetera. We shouldn't dread silence. We should become comfortable with it. Silence can be an incubator for wonderful insights and creative ideas, whether in the presence of others or when we are alone.

Shh!

Distractions vs. boredom

When people are idle, they often don't turn out well. Yet, idleness is part of what enables us to discover who we are beyond our mere physical forms or our roles in society.

Perhaps that's the paradox of idleness.

Staying all by ourselves and doing nothing is how we learn more about our own nature, but it's also when a never-ending flow of thoughts—often negative ones—attack us. The apparent idleness is only outside. Inside, it's all noise, confusion and a continuous flow of thoughts, memories and feelings.

One of the challenges of life might be to become wise enough to handle idleness and learn from it rather than letting it consume us.

On "perfect" communication

The same words often mean different things to different people. It's especially true for words that describe abstract concepts, such as:

- Work,
- Love,
- Truth,
- Religion,
- Philosophy,
- Value,
- Success,
- Happiness, and
- Money.

For instance, the word "work" evokes different images for different people. For some, work is what defines them, for others, it's what they do to pay the bills. For some, it's a joy, for others, it's a struggle.

"Love" can be romantic love, love for others, love for one's nation, unrequited love or unhealthy obsession with someone. In short, when people hear the word "love", different images spring to mind.

Each concept fills our mind with images, stories, and anecdotes while being connected to a set of beliefs unique to each of us. That's why the potential for miscommunication is endless.

The point is this. No matter how clear we are when we try to communicate, others may receive a different message from the one we intended. This is why communication is so hard, and working on our communication skills should be a never-ending process.

Trust is the foundation of society

If we lose trust in a relationship, the relationship starts dying.

If enough people lose trust in a currency, it becomes worthless.

If citizens lose trust in their politicians, unrest usually follows.

And if we don't trust ourselves, we lose self-respect and erode our self-esteem.

Trust is the foundation. We can't build anything substantial without it.

Creating vs. consuming

We are made to create. We feel better when we build intimate relationships, pursue exciting ventures or make something with our own hands. When we move from consuming to creating, we move from fleeting excitement to lasting fulfilment. Consuming often makes us feel restless and empty, while creating makes us feel content and proud. When we consume, we risk losing ourselves and burying our gifts. On the other hand, when we create, we express ourselves and start uncovering our gifts.

Let's try to create more.

The failed promise of consumption

We often consume to fill a void inside. We hope that whatever experience, service or product we buy will boost our status, make us more desirable and enable us to be more accepted.

But that void we feel inside can never be filled through consumption. Consuming leads us to forget about our true nature as creative beings. Often, we consume to distract ourselves from the act of creation because creating stuff is scary. What if the thing we create isn't good? What if we are not good enough? What if people don't like it? What if we receive criticism?

But can we afford not to create?

When we refuse to create, we refuse to express ourselves. We fail to use the creative process to learn about ourselves and discover our skills, talents and purpose. In doing so, we also refuse to serve the world by bringing our unique personality into it.

Through excessive consumption, we seek to forget—or even hope to overcome—our inadequacies, but that is an impossible task. It's only by embracing the creative process that we can face our fears head-on, learn about ourselves and reach a deeper sense of contentment.

Show me the incentive

We can often predict the behavior of people by looking at what motivates them. For instance:

- Politicians want to be reelected. As a result, they make empty promises, try to boost the economy artificially during the year of the elections or accept money from lobbies that will end up dictating their policies.
- Wall Street financial firms want people to invest their money with them and increase the amount of money they manage. It leads them to trade in and out of stocks often to show investors they're being active and to justify their hefty fees (even though it often leads to poor performance over the longer term).
- Shareholders are looking for short-term results. As a result, they might stop or slow down innovation and may prevent a CEO from executing his long-term vision in order to make short-term profits.
- Many CEOs want to stay in power but might not care that much about the long-term health of the company (unless they are the founder of the company). Because they're often compensated with stock options, they have a huge incentive to prop up the stock price, sometimes going against the long-term interest of investors or compromising the long-term perspective of the company.
- In general, employees want to make more money while

working less. Conversely, the employer wants them to work as hard as possible while paying them the bare minimum.

When we understand people's incentives, we can understand and, sometimes, predict their behavior. As the famous investor Charlie Munger said, "Show me the incentive and I will show you the outcome".

Environment and willpower

Our environment is more powerful than our willpower. We are weaker and far more pliable than we admit. While a supportive environment can turn us into wonderful human beings, under the wrong conditions and in the wrong place and time, we might have become Nazis, Japanese kamikazes, or criminals.

If you think you're any different, you're lying to yourself. It makes you a potential danger both to yourself and to others.

Illogical logic

Have you ever wondered why people around you do what they do? It may sometimes seem as though their behavior makes no sense. But it's usually our lack of perspective and our inability to put ourselves in their shoes that leads us to think this way.

People always act in a way that makes sense (to them). They have their own logic. If we could see everything that is going on in their mind—their hopes, dreams, fears, beliefs and past experiences—their actions would likely make more sense.

We simply lack perspective.

Many of the things we do are so that we can enjoy the present or improve our prospects. These things may help us reduce our anxiety or increase our sense of fulfilment. For instance, some people dream of buying a house while others want the freedom of renting. And from their perspective, they're both right and use their own "logic" to come to that conclusion.

The point is, there is no universal logic that would apply to everyone all the time. The decisions each individual makes must be seen in the proper context. It must encompass all their fears, aspirations and beliefs. For instance:

- Because something works for a lot of people doesn't mean it will work for us.
- Because a certain decision might help us make more money doesn't mean it's the most logical one.
- Because a strategy could help us scale our business doesn't mean it's what we should do.

When people say something is "logical", what they usually mean is that it makes sense to them. It's something they can stand behind or act upon, but they forget that it may not be the case for other people.

In the end, it's only "logical" if it makes sense to *us*. And since we're all different, the logical conclusion we arrive at may vary from one person to the next.

Everything is a trade-off

In a world where resources are limited, each of our actions comes with trade-offs. In other words, there is an opportunity cost with every decision we make. The opportunity cost is the idea that we can't do two things at the same time. The resources used on one thing can't be used on anything else. For instance:

- When we accept a job offer, we have to say no to every other potential job out there.
- When we are in one relationship, we shouldn't be in another relationship.
- When we study Spanish, we can't use the same hours to practice the piano.

In short, the fact that resources are limited forces us to make choices (i.e., trade-offs). Trade-offs aren't optional, they are the very essence of life.

The same goes for economic policies. Economics can be defined as the science of allocating scarce resources efficiently. Think about it this way: if resources were unlimited, economics would make no sense. We wouldn't need to work because all the resources would be unlimited. There would be no trade-offs because everything would be abundant. For instance, we wouldn't have to choose between a smaller house in the city center or a bigger house in the suburbs.

But that's not how things work in the real world. There are only so many beachfront properties. Because resources are limited, there is a need for trade-offs. We can't have it all. Let's take taxes for instance. The same money that goes into taxes can't go anywhere else. That is, the taxes corporations pay is money they can't reinvest to grow. Taxes individuals pay is money they don't have to buy products or services. And taxes used to fund education can't go into funding public hospitals.

In life, everything is a trade-off.

Inequality as a natural phenomenon

Some people operate under the premise that equality is the norm while inequality means something is wrong. But inequality is an inherent part of nature and an inevitable fact of life.

Nothing is equally distributed. Rivers, mountains, access to the sea, climate conditions, natural resources are all unevenly distributed across the globe. The same goes for natural disasters. For instance, Japan alone suffers about 20% of earthquakes with a magnitude of 6.0 or above. Hurricanes occur only in certain parts of the world. And the countries that are most prone to flood are almost all in Asia. And, of course, each person on this planet has a unique set of genes and life experience, which inherently generates inequality.

Inequality isn't a sign that something is wrong. It's not necessarily an indication that evil people are conspiring to keep others poor while enriching themselves.

In life, the default is inequality. We shouldn't be surprised when we see it everywhere. Of course, that isn't to say we shouldn't try to build societies where we all have the opportunities to reach our goals.

But we should expect inequalities to show up in many ways.

Utopians vs. visionaries

Utopians are delusional in that they deny an existing reality. As a result, everything they do is built on a foundation of sand. They have an idyllic vision that exists only in their mind. They believe the world should be different rather than accepting that the world is exactly as it should be. Instead of understanding why people act the way they do and trying to improve the world incrementally, they want to change people immediately. They assume that something is wrong with other people and that these other people need to be taught how to think properly. People who don't think the "right" way or disagree with them may end up disappearing sooner or later. Utopians are dangerous. They sell hell disguised as paradise.

On the other hand, visionaries see reality as it is. Then, they imagine how much better society could be. They act from an existing reality and seek to create a coherent plan of action to move toward their vision. Their plan takes human nature into account. They are pragmatic and grounded. They don't see pies in the sky.

Be a visionary, not a utopian. Be a positive force for society, not a destructive one. Aim to understand reality first. Then, act accordingly.

What doesn't change

People will always want to:

- Belong,
- Be happier,
- Be healthier,
- Be wealthier,
- Enjoy good food,
- Be better appreciated,
- Laugh and be entertained, and
- Acquire high-quality products that solve their problems at a fair price.

Let's keep that in mind.

Starting with what's true

There are few things we can be certain of. When trying to change our life, perhaps we can look at what appears to be true constantly for all (or most people) and start from there.

For instance, for most of us, it's better to:

- Have a job we love than a job we hate,
- Be healthy than unhealthy,
- Exercise than be sedentary,
- Have friends than be alone,
- Be skilled than have no skills,
- Be happy than sad, and
- Have some money than live in abject poverty.

If it seems to be both true most of the time for most people and beneficial, then perhaps that's where we should start.

Our progress as a species

We seldom appreciate the miracle that is peaceful co-existence. While there are terrible conflicts and tragedies happening around the world, the fact that millions of people live together relatively peacefully is astonishing. That's especially true considering we all have different opinions, values and political beliefs.

The default situation isn't peaceful human beings living together in harmony with nature and with each other. It's chaos, crime, murder, disease and poverty. We tend to forget that. Being able to co-exist peacefully at scale requires an extreme level of cooperation, tolerance and care for others.

It's a miracle.

Consequently, before saying the world is such a horrible place and humans are selfish creatures, perhaps we should remember where we're coming from. There are many issues that remain to be solved, but it doesn't mean we should deny the progress we've made as a species in the past few centuries.

24

ON MARKETING

Outstanding products or services are the ones that would still sell if marketing didn't exist. These are the products or services that people would happily use and recommend to their family and friends.

Marketing is often what enables companies to get away with providing inferior products or services. For many companies, marketing has become the art of selling substandard products at inflated prices to people who don't need them by playing on their insecurities or selling them hope.

Yet, in a world where billions of products exist and the size of the market is the entire world, marketing is needed for anyone who aspires to build a prosperous business. Enough people must know about our products to create the initial spark that will lead to sales. But a truly outstanding product or service might not need to be in that many hands before it can spread to more people. For instance:

- By getting a few thousand people to listen to our music, we have a shot at making it go viral.
- By getting an amazing book into the hands of a thousand ideal readers, we could increase our sales a hundredfold over time.

- By getting one hundred people to visit our delicious restaurant, we might generate enough word of mouth to grow our customer base significantly.

And if it doesn't work the first time, we can gather feedback and keep improving, or we can create another product and try again.

The bottom line is, often the product *is* the marketing. Its quality and usefulness should speak for itself.

The product is the marketing

Creating a product and figuring out how to sell it later seldom works. This is because true marketing happens at the product development level. The product sells itself because of the way it was conceived, the problem it solves and the intention behind it. For instance, you can't sell a bad book by designing a great cover and slapping a catchy title on it (unless you're a celebrity perhaps). Even if you spend millions and manage to sell hundreds of thousand of copies, you'll do so at a loss.

Perhaps we can think of marketing as an amplifier. When a product is a good market fit, marketing becomes easier. Marketing amplifies what works and makes the seller/producer more money. But when it's a bad market fit, marketing amplifies what doesn't work and ends up costing the producer a great deal of money in the long run.

Often, the problem is the product, and marketing alone may not be able to save it.

Product creation is an art, not a science

Most products or services are commercial failures. They are a huge time, money and energy pit. Everybody who tells you they have cracked the formula to creating a successful song, movie or training course is lying. There are many things we can do to improve our odds, but ultimately, there is an important element called "luck".

Therefore, it's useful to think of products or services as bets. If it works out, the payoff might be big. However, if it doesn't, we can reflect, learn and make another bet. The truth is most of the things we try won't work the first time. Most ventures will fail. But we shouldn't consider these as failures. They're merely feedback. Let's pick ourselves up, dust ourselves off and move on to the next opportunity.

25

ON WRITING

Clear writing is truth-seeking

Clear writing seeks to communicate the truth (our real intentions or feelings) while complex writing attempts to manipulate and confuse. Writing simple and clear sentences is difficult and requires many rewrites. When we write clearly, we have nowhere to hide—no fancy words, vague ideas or fluff. We're saying exactly what we mean, which can be scary.

The point is, clear writing is honest hard work, while unclear writing is disrespectful at best, manipulative at worst. Let's put ourselves in the shoes of whoever must read our words and spare them the suffering of bad and/or dishonest writing.

Thinking on paper

Writing is organized thinking. Everybody can think. Therefore, everybody can write. And the more we write and rewrite, the better we become at thinking.

Writers and time-traveling

Writing is sharing our thoughts through time. It is making our thinking and feelings available for the world to see now and in the future. As such, it is an extraordinary tool. Skilled writers can make a tremendous impact on the world around them and be read centuries after their death. As the stoic philosopher, Seneca, wrote two thousand years ago, "I have withdrawn not only from men, but from affairs, especially from my own affairs; I am working for later generations, writing down some ideas that may be of assistance to them."

Considering he's still being read two thousand years later, he is quite the time traveler.

Words matter

Words can be used to manipulate entire nations or inspire someone to make drastic changes in their life. The words we use or listen to can reshape our entire reality. People who seek to manipulate others rely on euphemisms, use vague words and tell people what they want to hear. They actively try to distort reality to push their own agenda.

Let's not be fooled.

THE POWER OF WORDS

Whoever can use words effectively can impact millions—for better or for worse.

The ultimate act of ego

We write because we want to be read. We seek to share our insights, beliefs or advice. We strive to influence our readers in some ways. Or we write to entertain. And in many cases, we have the desire—conscious or not—for our writing to be around long after we're gone. As we attempt to express our uniqueness, influence others or even become "immortal" through our writing, we commit what is perhaps the ultimate act of ego and self-preservation.

The "selfless" writer

While a writer may have a sincere desire to help, entertain or educate others, they can never be said to selfless. It leaves writers with a choice:

1. They can recognize that they're acting out of ego, or
2. They can believe they're acting selflessly.

In the first case, they accept that many of the things they say are merely a matter of opinion. They understand that they are probably wrong in some way or another. In the second case, they believe themselves and their message to be the ultimate truth. But where is such truth coming from? The universe? God? Their muse? A flash of insight during meditation? By believing that they can understand the "truth", they put themselves at the level of God, the Universe, Awareness, or whatever name we want to use. This isn't being selfless. This is being delusional.

The best we can hope for is to communicate our experiences, thoughts and intentions as truthfully as possible while knowing that they aren't the whole truth. But let us not delude ourselves in thinking we're speaking the undeniable truth.

26

ON MAKING AN IMPACT

The wise and the foolish

Wise people seek to understand the world before trying to improve it. Fools seek to change the world without understanding it.

Wise people have a shot at making an impact. Fools are likely to make a mess.

The power of strategy

Working hard might double our productivity.

A good strategy can improve our results tenfold.

An excellent strategy could increase our impact a hundredfold.

Good vs. great strategy

A good strategy tells us what to do. A great strategy tells us what *not* to do. It shortens the distance between point A, where we are, and point B, where we want to be, by eliminating unnecessary activities and removing distractions.

Sometimes, the most important thing is knowing what *not* to do.

Making a difference

Many people say they want to make a difference in the world, but they merely want to make more money, become famous, be loved or gather accolades to make them feel better about themselves.

The most powerful forces on earth

As humans, love, compassion, faith, gratitude, humility and desire might be the biggest assets we have.

Love is the willingness to accept others and give them the space to grow to their full potential.

Compassion is the ability to place ourselves in other people's shoes and see things from their perspective. Accumulating a variety of experiences enables us to go beyond black-and-white thinking and have a more nuanced vision of the way the world works.

Faith is our ability to see what's not there yet and move toward it despite uncertainty and fear. The paradox of faith is that we often need to believe in something without having reason to—without having proof.

Gratitude is the ability to appreciate all we have. It's the feeling that we're already complete, that we've already "won". Having our cup full enables us to give more to others and to share our gifts and express our personality more deeply.

Humility is the willingness to accept that we never know as much as we think we do, that there is always something to learn from other people or from the experiences we have.

Desire is the urge to pursue a certain endeavor—a calling, a particular interest or a cause we want to contribute to.

There are many things that we can do to live a good life, but cultivating more love, compassion, faith, gratitude, humility and desire will usually help us make the most of our time on this planet.

Everything is energy

If we aspire to have a meaningful impact on the world, we must come to terms with the fact that everything is energy. If we want to scale our impact, we must learn to channel as much energy as possible.

Let's look at some of the levers we have access to:

- Money (stored energy). Money is time and effort that was accumulated from creating and selling a product or service. It is stored energy.
- Other people's time (borrowed energy). Our time or the time of other people is energy. For instance, when we hire people or work with contractors or freelancers, we use their time so that we have access to more energy to accomplish more things.
- Focus (channeled energy). Focus can be seen as channeled energy. For instance, we can produce far more energy by focusing on one key task for an extensive period than by jumping from one task to another every few minutes.
- Knowledge (curated energy). Today's knowledge is the accumulation of past experiences and wisdom curated for their effectiveness and usefulness. If something stands the test of time, it usually does so for a reason. The more we can tap into that knowledge, the more we can increase the amount of energy at our disposal.
- Technology (multiplied energy). Technology multiplies energy through leverage. For instance, the internet enables us to reach millions of people just by posting a video where in the past such reach would have been almost impossible for the average person.

The more energy we accumulate, the more productive we become and the more impact we can have.

IMPOSSIBLE IS SUBJECTIVE

We can never know what we're capable of unless we give it a try.

What's impossible for us today may be possible tomorrow.

We all evolve and learn.

Therefore, impossible is subjective.

27

ON STRIVING TO BE A GOOD PERSON

The dog-eat-dog world

We can see this world as a dog-eat-dog world. Or we can strive to build win-win relationships with anyone we come into contact. It all depends on what we believe to be true about the world.

Sometimes, what we believe about the world is what we seek, and what we seek is what we end up finding.

Life's biggest challenge

One of life's biggest challenges is to keep our heart pure, our intentions noble and our motivation untainted as we face criticisms, setbacks and disappointments—i.e., we don't want to kill the playful and curious child within us.

Happy are those who can keep their sense of curiosity and wonder about the world intact as they grow old and/or become successful and famous.

The importance of friendships

Do not wait for someone to put fuel on the fire of friendship. Proactively contact people you love being around and make sure you meet them on a regular basis. Share more of yourself with them. Strive to nurture the relationship and see if others feel the same.

Having friends is one of the most important things in life. This is even truer as we get older.

Networking vs. making friends

Traditional networking is often the art of pretending to care about other people so that we can use them to reach our goals. Instead of networking, why not become friends with people whose values and goals align with ours and see what unfolds?

Let's not network, let's build genuine friendships with people we care about and want to hang out with. This will lead to fruitful collaborations in the future.

Humility and arrogance

Humility is seeing ourselves as part of the whole.

Arrogance is seeing ourselves as better than the whole.

Being good people

We don't need to be religious to be good people. Being religious doesn't automatically make us good people. In truth, we know what we should and shouldn't do. Below are common-sense rules:

- Don't cheat.
- Don't steal.
- Don't hurt people.
- Avoid lying or manipulating others.
- Be kind.
- Stay humble.

In other words, let's not do to others what we wouldn't want others to do to us. In most situations, this golden rule will guide us toward the right decision.

Praying daily, going to church on Sundays, broadcasting how pious we are or how much we love God. None of these things means anything. What matters is how we behave with others and what our intentions are.

If we break the fundamental rules that make us decent human beings, our so-called religiosity is questionable, at the very least.

Being "spiritual" isn't an excuse

Spirituality is often a tool that "spiritual" people use to spread unprovable ideas. It enables them to justify any action (good or bad) and get away with it.

The law of attraction is a good example. If we get the results we want, it's proof that it works. And if we don't, it's because we didn't believe hard enough. In either case, the law of attraction wins. Now, that doesn't mean there isn't an ounce of truth in it but merely that we can't disprove it.

The bottom line is, spirituality isn't an excuse to escape our responsibility, sell questionable products or services, or manipulate others for our own benefit. And it's certainly not an excuse to avoid any type of rational thinking.

In short, being "spiritual", like being "religious", is not an excuse to be less than a decent human being. If anything, it should lead us to expect far more of ourselves.

Seeking spiritual enlightenment

We should not pursue spiritual enlightenment unless we feel a strong calling for it. If we merely like "the idea" of it, our ego will make it yet another thing to strive for, another thing to possess. And it will use spirituality for its self-aggrandizement. It will turn into one more thing we do to acquire a better status and make us feel superior.

Humility, open-mindedness, curiosity and the desire to seek the truth should be our main drivers. If we pursue spirituality for any other reason, we'll probably go astray.

RAISING OUR LEVEL OF CONSCIOUSNESS

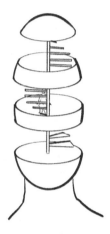

Perhaps our only goal in life is to raise our level of consciousness
and invite others to do the same.

CONCLUSION

Living a meaningful life that we can be proud of is difficult. It requires self-awareness, courage, curiosity, continuous improvement and a great dose of humility. During our life, we must reinvent ourselves as our situation evolves. We must upgrade our sense of self and let go of ideas and beliefs that don't serve us anymore. Sometimes, we must cut ties with people from whom we've grown apart.

Living is an art, not a science. The "do this, and you'll get that" mentality only applies in a minority of situations. Most of the time, the best answer is that it depends on the circumstances. That's why no book can tell us how to live our lives, and no "guru" can decide for us what our life should be. We must act and reflect on our actions to create the feedback loop we need to move closer to our ideal life.

In this book, I've attempted to point out a few elements that may help nourish your personal reflection. I have shared my thoughts on a variety of topics that I deemed worth writing about. Whenever possible, I've tried to go against the grain and challenge common clichés or bring more nuance to complex topics.

My sincere hope is that you have benefited from reading this book by gaining some insights, discovering new perspectives or learning something about yourself or about human nature.

As for me, I'm looking forward to revisiting this book ten years from now and seeing how my views have changed (quite a bit I suspect).

I will conclude by reminding you that wherever you are now isn't where you will be tomorrow. When in doubt, we should let the following forces assist us during our time on earth:

Gratitude, humility and self-compassion.

These forces alone will go a long way to help you live a meaningful life.

In other words, as you wake up each day, remember how blessed you are to be granted another day (gratitude). Use that day to learn more about yourself and the world (humility). And, while doing so, make sure you are kind to yourself (self-compassion).

We're all doing the best we can, where we are, with what we have.

Let's remember that truth as we move through life.

With love,

Thibaut Meurisse

ABOUT THE AUTHOR

THIBAUT MEURISSE

Thibaut is the author of over 20 books including "Master Your Emotions" which has sold over 400,000 copies and has been translated into more than 30 languages including French, Spanish, German, Chinese, Thai, and Portuguese.

Thibaut's mission is to help ordinary people attain extraordinary results.

If you like simple practical and inspiring books, and are committed to improve your life, you'll love his work.

thibautmeurisse.com
thibaut.meurisse@gmail.com

OTHER BOOKS BY THE AUTHORS:

Mastery Series

1. Master Your Emotions: A Practical Guide to Overcome Negativity and Better Manage Your Feelings

2. Master Your Motivation: A Practical Guide to Unstick Yourself, Build Momentum and Sustain Long-Term Motivation

3. Master Your Focus: A Practical Guide to Stop Chasing the Next Thing and Focus on What Matters Until It's Done

4. Master Your Destiny: A Practical Guide to Rewrite Your Story and Become the Person You Want to Be

5. Master Your Thinking: A Practical Guide to Align Yourself with Reality and Achieve Tangible Results in the Real World

6. Master Your Success: Timeless Principles to Develop Inner Confidence and Create Authentic Success

7. Master Your Beliefs: A Practical Guide to Stop Doubting Yourself and Build Unshakeable Confidence

8. Master Your Time: A Practical Guide to Increase Your Productivity and Use Your Time Meaningfully

9. Master Your Learning: A Practical Guide to Learn More Deeply, Retain Information Longer and Become a Lifelong Learner

10. Master Your Decisions: A Practical Guide to Make Better Decisions Faster and Stack the Odds in Your Favor

Productivity Series

1. Dopamine Detox: A Short Guide to Remove Distractions and Get Your Brain to Do Hard Things

2. Immediate Action: A 7-Day Plan to Overcome Procrastination and Regain Your Motivation

3. Powerful Focus: A 7-Day Plan to Develop Mental Clarity and Build Strong Focus

4. Strategic Mindset: A 7-Day Plan to Identify What Matters and Create a Strategy that Works

Other books

Crush Your Limits: Break Free from Limitations and Achieve Your True Potential

Do The Impossible: How to Become Extraordinary and Impact the World at Scale

Goal Setting: The Ultimate Guide to Achieving Life-Changing Goals

Habits That Stick: The Ultimate Guide to Building Habits That Stick Once and For All

Productivity Beast: An Unconventional Guide to Getting Things Done

The Greatness Manifesto: Overcome Your Fear and Go After What You Really Want

The One Goal: Master the Art of Goal Setting, Win Your Inner Battles, and Achieve Exceptional Results

The Passion Manifesto: Escape the Rat Race, Uncover Your Passion and Design a Career and Life You Love

The Thriving Introvert: Embrace the Gift of Introversion and Live the Life You Were Meant to Live

The Ultimate Goal Setting Planner: Become an Unstoppable Goal Achiever in 90 Days or Less

Upgrade Yourself: Simple Strategies to Transform Your Mindset, Improve Your Habits and Change Your Life

Success is Inevitable: 17 Laws to Unlock Your Hidden Potential, Skyrocket Your Confidence and Get What You Want From Life

Wake Up Call: How To Take Control Of Your Morning And Transform Your Life

Made in the USA
Las Vegas, NV
22 November 2024

12411013R00125